Maximize Publishing Inc. Presents:

The Newborn Entrepreneur

Changing the World One Person at A Time

By: Dr. Michael McCain

The Newborn Entrepreneur

Maximize Publishing Inc.

2018 Monterey Ave

Bronx N.Y. 10457

Attn.: Michael McCain

C/o: Kevin Brown

ISBN-13:
978-0615816111 (Maximize Publishing Inc.)

ISBN-10:
0615816118

The Newborn Entrepreneur

The Newborn Entrepreneur

Changing the World One Person at A Time

By: Dr. Michael McCain

The Newborn Entrepreneur

Table of Contents:

The Newborn Entrepreneur

Why I Wrote This Book:

"How many people are completely successful in every department of life? Not one. The most successful people are the ones who learn from their mistakes and turn their failures into opportunities."
– Zig Ziglar

For anyone who has ever read any of my books you would know that I am all about inspiring people to live their best life and to achieve their goals successfully. With that in mind my vision writing The Newborn Entrepreneur is not far from the same of any other literary work of mine. I read allot about entrepreneurship and participate in dozens of networking events per year. Many new emerging business owners and leaders have participated in life coaching or business coaching consultations or strategy meetings with me. I've taken my most common advice an answers talked about in these sessions to comprise this book.

The Newborn Entrepreneur

I want to encourage every new entrepreneur to peruse their vision and their goals. With the changing and evolving world economy for some creating and starting a business is becoming as easy as a click of a button! Some of us are holding our business right at our fingertips with our high-tech phones and gadgets. Needless to say how social media has forever changed the way people conduct business and communicate. I am encouraged and empowered that the times are creating opportunity for more people to take control of their future and make their dreams come true!

Building a business is definitely not an easy task; entrepreneurship and business is a process most people dread and try hard to avoid. Many are fearful of venturing into business for fear of the challenges involved and that's why so many people prefer to remain employees. So for the first time business owner who's a neophyte, to the more experience business masterminds this book will be a great encouragement and source of strength.

Building a successful business from scratch is simply all about surmounting business challenges; nothing more and nothing less.

The Newborn Entrepreneur

Anyone in business will tell you it's never a smooth ride. Yet the freedom of owning your own business is liberating and rewarding. It takes mentorship, education, a right plan, self-motivation and strategy, just to name a few pointers. Every entrepreneur knows you can never become satisfied at your present level, you must keep climbing what I call "the success mountain" until you reach your peak and potential. There's always room for growth, improvement and revision. Every successful entrepreneur will revisit those stages time and time again.

In business you will face many challenges, disappointments and even failures. How you handle those challenges, disappointments and failures will determine how successful you become and the altitude that you will reach. There are countless CEO's who were high school and college dropouts who later became millionaires and billionaires. They failed countless times at attempts to get just one opportunity to work out in their favor. The challenge here is when you have a dream more powerful than failure or closed doors it will push you to find your yes!

You may be facing some closed doors but your breakthrough might be waiting right on the other side. You may face 1000 no's before maybe, to eventually arrive to "yes". You have to know that your "yes" is out there and stay diligent until you arrive to finish line. You have to refuse to give up, be self-motivated and goal orientated. A college degree does not guarantee a successful business. There are countless people with minimal next to no formal education who become successful at what they do and make substantial money. You can be one of those top entrepreneurs and business men and women.

Foreword:
-Brion E. Nelson

There is an emerging trend in the world, especially in the United States amid an economic recession and little to no opportunities that provide personal fulfillment, satisfaction and rewards, that is gaining immense momentum and redefining the times and age. This trend is none other than Entrepreneurship.

What is an entrepreneur you ask? Have you ever seen one? How would you know what one would look like? Talk like or even act like? The answer is simple. You see one every day. Entrepreneurship is actively involved in everyday life from the places you go, to the assets and devices you use and down to the things you watch. Entrepreneurship and entrepreneurs are everywhere.

An entrepreneur is a specially gifted individual with vision, passion, innovation and the tangible and intangible attributes and resources that propel them to fulfill their life. They are the backbone of the business world, responsible for some of the greatest businesses, inventions and assets known. Entrepreneurs define the age, epoch, times and culture through their vision and innovative creativity. Entrepreneurs are visionaries, leaders and pioneers who see opportunity to be utilized, seize the moment and use their innovative creativity to affect the culture. Entrepreneurs are trailblazers, pioneers, leaders and innovators who are persistent, determined and resourceful.

In this time of economic downturn, especially in the era of globalization, there is a greater demand for entrepreneurship. There is a demand for refreshing innovation and a demand for individuals who will trail blaze and path find, exploring new possibilities while pioneering change, innovation and new ways of thinking and living. In fact one of the greatest surges of activity in any economy is entrepreneurship and there is no greater beckoning for entrepreneurs than now. Even entrepreneurs are reinvented every so often to reinvent the times and now more than ever more entrepreneurs are starting to emerge.

Ever since I was 13 years of age, I was always intrigued with entrepreneurship, the freedom, the creativity, the innovation, the value and the benefit of self-fulfillment. I even took classes in high school and went to Johnson & Wales to graduate with my B.S. in entrepreneurship. Now at the age of 21 God has graced me with the wisdom, the ability and the passion in my own venture, Kingdom Enterprise in addition to many other small ventures, programs, goods and services, etc.

I believe that entrepreneurship is one of the greatest concepts ever borne. As an entrepreneur I live outside the box, perform outside the lines and against the status quo, seeking to establish my own culture and values. My definition of being an entrepreneur is to be unique, innovative and creative; maximize every talent and ability to the maximum capacity and value; to make every idea and vision a reality and ultimately to live life self-fulfilled while inspiring others to do the same.

Entrepreneurs inspire the entrepreneurial spirit in others. Many people have always wanted to start their own business or function; they sometimes never had the motivation, the courage or even the knowledge of how to perform. This is why this book "The Newborn Entrepreneur" is so critical and a motivational tool to boost confidence, provide insight and encourage any and all to pursue their vision and goals for satisfaction and self-fulfillment.

I have had the pleasure of working with Michael McCain, who to me is one of the savviest individuals with an entrepreneurial spirit that I have ever come into contact with. "The Newborn Entrepreneur "is a must read for all entrepreneurs, aspiring business owners, business men and women and anyone looking to be inspired. If you ever wanted more in life or to take that step of faith that before you never had the ability, this book will surely motivate you not to take a step of faith, but a leap.

McCain does a terrific job defining what an entrepreneur is, highlighting the benefits and the sacrifices of such a lifestyle. He offers insightful counsel on how to motivate yourself to pursue your dreams, stay inspired and develop a passion for the things you love to do. No true entrepreneur is satisfied with an outcome or level. They always strive and desire more, scuba diving deeper; going farther and climbing higher on what he so eloquently calls "the success mountain".

"The Newborn Entrepreneur" encourages all to break through and stay inspired although an entrepreneur may get numerous "no's", hundreds of "maybes" and few "yes's". But the book coaches all to keep pursuing persistently because there is an inevitable "yes" and that "yes" will outweigh all the "no's" and "maybes".

For all looking for more and for satisfaction on a different pattern that they have not yet attained, for all that need that thrust and push that before they didn't have, you are reading the right book at the right time. This literary work will help you discover the entrepreneur in you , inspire you to rediscover your passion and give you the tools, keys and confidence to persistently pursue your dreams and conquer every obstacle along the way as you embark on a journey to a new frontier as a new trailblazer, a new pathfinder and as "The Newborn Entrepreneur."

The Newborn Entrepreneur

My Journey as an Entrepreneur

Chapter One:

"The height attained by great men is not by sudden flight. For while their companions lay asleep, these men were toiling in the night."

– Anonymous

Like most full-blooded entrepreneurs I got my start early in life. For most of my life I can honestly say I have not had to work for anyone other than myself. From the age of 14 I started working. At the time I was a foster child and started working summer youth employment, a program every teenager in New York looked forward to in their early teens. I can remember both the pressure by my peers and even my foster mom to make sure I applied for my working papers on time and also having my medical records up to part so I can be ready to work for the summer.

Working was something I loved doing, learning new things, meeting new people and building skills for the present and future. My first summer employment job was at Upper Manhattan Mental Health Center on 145th and Amsterdam Ave. New York, N.Y. It was there I learned how to work with mentally challenged children, moved my way up from working with children to working with recovering addicts in the Alcoholism Unit. Data processing, filing papers and communication skills was what I learned. While working, I used my pay check to start a gift basket business where I took my 800 dollar summer youth check and turned it into a 3,500 dollar a week income.

I had no assistant, and needless to say an extra 3,500 dollars was excellent for a 14 year old with no bills and responsibilities. I ate lunch out every day while my co-workers bagged lunch and maybe ate out once a week. My foster mom began to be concerned about where I was making all this extra money from considering I was only 14 years old.
Eventually I had to let her in on my secret as she began to investigate supposing I was selling drugs. After finding out it was all honest

hard earned money, she was not only shocked but proud.

The biggest mistake I made was not having a plan for my money. I earned roughly if not more than 30,000 that summer. Spent it on eating out every day, clothes for back to school, cabs everywhere I went, because I did not believe in walking. Treating my friends out to dinner, lunch or allowing them to borrow money I never saw again. While these were my early mistakes most adults are presently making them. At that age with a 30,000 dollar plus income in 2 months I could have greatly changed my future with a greater plan.

Another interesting fact was my spending habits were not anything shy of that I saw my foster mom's spending habits were. Now I am not blaming her, I take full responsibility for my own mistakes but it's no wonder where I learned to be so free hearted with money. Her example in spending money was not always a good one; hence my spending habits were not far off. Needless to say my business had highs and lows and soon altogether collapsed.

When I turned 18 I started a new business, this time with a little more savvy than the first go round. I was old enough to incorporate, called one of my best friends at the time and made him my business partner. Started a cleaning business, I had a personal clientele with the seniors from my church who would call me every week to run errands and clean or fix things they were unable to do. I knew I could transform what I was doing into greater income and I did!

My business partner and I started the business with 350 dollars and an additional 200 we spent on flyers, ink, business cards and stamps. We marketed our business every week. My first 500 calls were all for jobs! While I would have loved to be able to hire someone my focus was finding clients so I could work. I took a chance at mailing my flyer and cover letter to a well-known millionaire preacher in New York. By the age of 21 I was now working for a millionaire with a contract. I loved my work, I loved the growth of my business, yet I quickly became too comfortable with my millionaire client.

The mistake I made was no longer looking for new business, stopped advertising, closed other contracts with clients because they were not paying me as much as my millionaire clients. While the pay was good, I could have done better. I could have hired other help for the smaller jobs and grew my business to the point of where I would not have to work myself. I was all mixed up; I think I enjoyed the experience of being in a rich neighborhood in Manhattan, visiting mansions in New Jersey and meeting famous people. While I was not star struck I was in a learning process that a college degree would not give me. I was soaking in everything I could and it molded me and changed me in to a better business man and entrepreneur.

"For every failure, there's an alternative course of action. You just have to find it. When you come to a road block, take a detour."
– Mary Kay Ash

Now how many of us have made decisions and choices in life that we wish we could go back edit and change. If I were able to hear your response I am sure it would be YES! We have all made some choices that landed us in never, never land; not because we wanted to end up their but because circumstances and events landed us there. I want you to know that every mistake I made on my journey to being an entrepreneur was worth it. Sometimes we like to say if I could turn back the hands of time and start over knowing what I have learned I would be alright. While that may be true, I would never want to go back because then I wouldn't be here!

"I successfully started and failed at a few businesses built from scratch. What I love about the entrepreneurial process is this; no matter what level of success or fame I attain today or tomorrow, the thought of my early days in life, when I had absolutely nothing will always keep me humble"

-Michael McCain

When I look back on where I came from in comparison with where I am at this moment I can honestly say everything I have been through and experienced was well worth it! Every mistake I made taught me valuable lessons. As a matter of fact some of my most valuable lessons in life all involved loss or money. While I always knew I was born for greatness I could not shake the fact that I made terrible mistakes along the way. Most of my mistakes came from the fact I had no mentors, no one to speak the wisdom I needed until I met my millionaire clients while I was operating my cleaning business.

All it really takes is one wise person in your life to shift you into a whole new dimension mentally, geographically and physically. I can remember standing for hours talking with my mentor, I was fixed like glue soaking up every word the man and his friends had to say. The reason being was because I was so appreciative that someone was willing to take a moment out of their busy life to speak some wisdom into mine. Not to mention the fact that they were doing it for free when there were countless hundreds to thousands of people who had to pay thousands of dollars for counseling sessions and advice with this millionaire preacher.

The Newborn Entrepreneur

The Makings of An Entrepreneur

Chapter Two:

The true process and making of an entrepreneur is humbling but it's truly up to the person to hold on to the morals and values that the experience teaches them. The makings of an entrepreneur include misunderstanding from family and friends who have not a clue about the vision that you have before you. Don't let that stop you, keep pressing. The makings of an entrepreneur also include sacrifices of time, money and energy to put into making a business, brand or product successful. So with that in mind let's ponder the question, what makes an entrepreneur?

What makes an entrepreneur is the question at hand. It certainly helps to have strong technology skills or expertise in a key area yet these are not the key defining characteristics of entrepreneurship. Of course it takes great skill to build a business. Yet entrepreneurs need more than just skill, there are thousands of people and even potentially millions that all have the same skill or ability as you might have. What will set you out to be different among them all is your ability to capture and reach your target market. Some of the key qualities that an entrepreneur needs are traits such as creativity, the ability to keep going in the face of hardship, and the social skills needed to build teams and fulfill leadership roles.

Not every entrepreneur is a great leader, but must have some skill set to lead a team, small group or operate in a place of leadership that can run a business in the direction it needs to go. They must be able to stand their ground, mean what they say, manage their problems and trials that the business may face and not fold under the pressure. If you want to start a business, it's essential to learn the specific skills that underpin these qualities. It's also important to develop entrepreneurial skills if you're in a job role where you're expected to develop a business, or "take things forward" more generally.

In this chapter, we will be looking at the skills you need to be a successful entrepreneur, and we'll explore resources that you can use to develop the traits needed for success. Remember that exploring entrepreneurship is a joy but there are some key things a person can do to enhance their career and skill, they need to identify the traits of an entrepreneur, strengthen those traits and weak areas and begin the process of what I call "the makings of en entrepreneur".

The Newborn Entrepreneur

Defining The Art of Entrepreneurship

We don't open up the conversation enough to what entrepreneurship really is. In fact, most of the time we spend allot of time defining it by some new trend we see someone doing, but many of us do not see that we ourselves have enough skill within us for entrepreneurial pursuit. Some experts think of entrepreneurs as people who are willing to take risks that other people are not. Others define them as people who start and build successful businesses.

Thinking about the first of these definitions, entrepreneurship doesn't necessarily involve starting your own business. Many people who don't work for themselves are recognized as entrepreneurs within their organizations. Someone who has entrepreneurial skill are usually people that have great skill and expertise, with that skill and expertise the person is able to advance within the company and open an opportunity to earn more money.

When you tap into the entrepreneur philosophy and mindset you will shift yourself into a place where you think from a place of increase, productivity, strategy, problem solving, branding, marketing, enhancement and difference. Now ask yourself the question right here and now with those traits does it mean that a person has to start a business to be an entrepreneur? In case your unaware, the answer is no. You don't need to start a business of your own, yet you do have enough skill if you fit the mold of what I describe to be successful at it.

Regardless of how you define an "entrepreneur," one thing is certain: becoming a successful entrepreneur isn't easy. You become successful when you provide a service that people can't live without. You become successful when you solve problems and build strategies that no one else seems to be able to do. When you tap into that place you will change your income and your outcome. That goes for the person who starts a business down to the person who just uses their skill to enhance someone else's business.

So, how does one person successfully take advantage of an opportunity, while another, equally knowledgeable person does not? Do entrepreneurs have a different genetic makeup? Or do they operate from a different vantage point, which somehow directs their decisions for them?

Though many researchers have studied the subject, there are no definitive answers. For every entrepreneur who pursues business their reasons for doing so are all different. Most entrepreneurs I have been privilege to meet were people who grew up in poverty, they had an adverse reaction to it and made sure that they did everything in their power to use what God gave them to bring themselves into a better place. The same can be said of those who stumbled into success like a freak accident. Some people were so busy working on their skill and enhancing their work. They were so engulfed with educating themselves and learning that they had no idea that their habit would lead them into success. I want to ask you do you have a personal habit that can be building a secret success muscle in your life.

So what really makes a successful entrepreneur? What gives entrepreneurs the passion and drive to make the accomplishments and success that they achieve? What we do know is that successful entrepreneurs seem to have certain traits in common.

We've gathered these traits into seven categories:

- Personal characteristics.
- Creativity (Imagination)
- Interpersonal skills.
- Relentless faith

The Newborn Entrepreneur

- Critical and creative thinking skills.
- Practical skills.
- Hunger for learning

Let's put these components under a microscope and see what the ingredients to a successful entrepreneur are all made of. While we go more in depth take time to ask yourself if you want to become a successful entrepreneur.

Personal Characteristics & Creativity/ Imagination:

First take a moment to examine your personal characteristics, values and beliefs. Do you have an entrepreneur mindset? Do you have some of the character traits and makings of typical successful entrepreneurs?

1.   Optimism: are you an optimistic thinker? There is such a thing as optimism and pessimistic. People who think from an Optimistic mindset see the success, the good and the invisible. They are excellent at finding the good in everything and usually have that outlook about most things in life, while the opposite of that is pessimistic. A pessimistic mindset worries about the "what if" too much and the negativity they see.

When you are an entrepreneur the ability to be an optimistic thinker is a great asset. When you are optimistic it will help you in the process of the makings and molding of your business, because it may take you a while as a neonate entrepreneur to find yourself and to discover your flow and tap into your potential. When you are optimistic it helps brighten even the darkest moments, every entrepreneur needs to develop this trait.

2.   Creativity and Imagination go hand and hand with optimism. When you are creative you trust that the vision you see before you is real. You have no physical evidence of its existence other than the download to your mind and spirit that it can happen. With that thought/imagination you have to bring yourself into a place of planning and strategy to bring that vision and dream to pass.

3.   Vision: Do you have an eye to easily see where things can be improved? Are you the type of person who has the ability to quickly "grasp the big picture," and articulately be able to communicate a vision or plan to people who need to carry it out? Do you have the ability to create a compelling vision of the future and put it

together with such excellence that you can inspire others to engage with that vision?

4.   Initiative: Are you able to take responsibility of solving problems, creating strategies and finding answers to hard questions? Business and everyday people need someone with a skill set like this and anyone who possesses it has the ability to bring improvement to people's personal lives as well as to a corporate structure of business both small and large.

5.   Interpersonal Skills: Are you a people person? Do you work well with others? People who possess interpersonal skills make increase in business with very little effort. Some call it the gift of gab, while others call it effective communication skills no matter what you may decide to call it; it is a skill that is an asset to any entrepreneur.

6.   Relentless Faith: Are you timid? Do you bend at the first sign of trouble? If so, you may have to get rid of those qualities quickly. Because to be a successful entrepreneur you need to have relentless faith. You need to be in a place where in spite of what you see you don't bend. You don't let the events of life and things happen in or out of your business to affect you in a way that may result in failure or giving up.

Having relentless faith also means that your passion, vision and hunger for your success have to be strong enough to weather any storm that may present itself or oppose your destiny. You have to be relentless in the face of opposition knowing that you're going to fully come out of what your experiencing you just need to hold on a little while until your lifeline comes in.

7.   Desire To Lead: Are you a person who enjoys being in charge and making decisions? Are you motivated to lead others? This is a quality that entrepreneurs need to have to be successful. We all know that there are plenty of people that want to lead for their own selfish reasons, but the real question is do you really have skill to lead honestly and out of a pure heart. Some people start off well and then the power trip takes them to another place. The question to ask yourself when you go into entrepreneurship and business is; can you handle power? Can you handle influence? Can you handle leading? When you have found the answers to these questions you will then get to the bottom of your true intention to lead.

You have to lead by intention, you have to lead knowing that your heart is pure and you have a real passion and desire to see your business, employees, clients and partners be successful. When you have a heart for your business and people you work with or work for you will quickly lead that people pick up on that and respond better when they know there in good hands.

8.   Critical & Creative Thinking Skills: What is your mind worth? How good is your thinking? Do you have good thinking skills? It is largely assumed that most entrepreneurs have good thinking skills and that is where there success comes from. Yet the truth is some people find that success by chance. They just so happened to be working on something and developed a skill, product or service that people really needed. Then there are those who have brilliant minds that develop concepts and ideas that become powerful.

So what is your mind worth? Do you have a million dollar idea sitting inside of you? Of course you do. Do you have a million dollar product inside of you? Of course you do. Do you have a million dollar service inside of you? Of course you do!!! It's largely up to you to stimulate your mind to cultivating and creating strategies and answers that will both reward you and those who need you most. You have to cultivate and create thinking skills.

If you suffer from boredom it is a sign to you that you're not living in purpose. How many times do you sit and say to your-self "I am bored?" I believe we have all said it at some point or other in our lives. Boredom is a sign that your mind is un-stimulated. You are sitting idle or being idle about your purpose. The truth be told when most people say they are bored, there's always something to do, they just don't want to do what needs to be done. I have been a victim of saying " I am bored", but I had books to write, books to edit, paper work that needed to be done, phone calls to make, important emails to respond to, a home to clean, family members to spend quality time with.

So the truth is you have to stimulate your mind, give yourself some inspiration to walk out your destiny, purposes and plans. Feed your mind with something valuable and watch your purpose and success start budding before your eyes!

9.   Drive and Persistence:

In entrepreneurship you have to have your own get up and go you cannot always wait for motivating moments or rely on others around you to motivate you. The question is, are you self-motivated and energetic? Are you prepared to put in the work that would be required for you to meet your goals?

10. Risk Tolerance:

Are you able to take risks? Everyone knows that entrepreneurship comes along with risk. It's often looked at as a gamble because there's no guarantee sometimes how profits or losses will go. Do you have a tolerance for risk? Are you able to take risks, and make decisions when facts are uncertain?

11. Resilience:

Are you resilient? Are you able to pick yourself up when things don't go as planned? Are you able to learn and grow from your mistakes and failures? (People who avoid taking action because they are afraid of failing need to work hard to overcome the fear of FAILURE. You need to face your fears and move forward.) Needless to say your fears will not only cripple you but hold your business back from reaching its potential and success.

Interpersonal Skills

As a successful entrepreneur, you'll have to work closely with people – this is where it is critical to be able to **build great**

relationships with your team, customers, suppliers, shareholders, investors, and more. Some people are more gifted in this area than others, but, fortunately, you can learn and improve these skills. The types of interpersonal skills you'll need I have outlined at the end of this chapter:

- Leadership and Motivation: Can you **lead** and **motivate others** to follow you and deliver your vision? And are you able to **delegate** work to others? As a successful entrepreneur, you'll have to depend on others to get beyond a very early stage in your business – there's just too much to do all on your own!

- Communication Skills: Are you competent with all types of **communication**? You need to be able to communicate well to sell your vision of the future to investors, potential clients, team members, and more. Listening: Do you hear what others are telling you? Your ability to listen can make or break you as an entrepreneur. Make sure that you're skilled at **active listening** and **empathetic listening**.

- Personal Relations: Are you **Emotionally Intelligent**? The higher you're EI (Emotional Intelligence), the easier it will be for you to work with others. The good news is that you can improve your emotional intelligence!

• Negotiation: Are you a good **negotiator**? Not only do you need to negotiate keen prices, you also need to be able to resolve differences between people in a positive, mutually beneficial way. You will need negotiating skills for settling issues with clients and customers as well as handling day to day business affairs and expenses.

• Ethics: Do you deal with people based on respect, **integrity**, fairness, and truthfulness? Can you lead **ethically**? You'll find it hard to build a happy, committed team if you deal with people – staff, customers or suppliers – in a snappy or nonchalant way.

Your interpersonal skills are a part of the foundation leading into how you conduct business and how you will be received in business. Can you identify the areas where you need work? Can you identify the areas that are your strengths? Either way you must know your strengths and weaknesses in moving forward in obtaining your success.

Power to Create & Skill to Manage

Chapter Three:

Critical and Creative Thinking Skills

As an entrepreneur, you also need to come up with fresh ideas, and make good decisions about opportunities and potential projects. You have to be quick witted and willing to stand out from the crowd. You have to be daring to be unique and willing to use your difference as a way to market and gain the attention of clients and customers. Many people think that you're either born creative or you're not. However, creativity is a skill that you can develop if you invest the time and effort.

•　·Creative Thinking: Are you able to see situations from a variety of perspectives and come up with original ideas? (There are many **creativity tools** that will help you do this.)

•　Problem Solving: How good are you at coming up with sound solutions to the problems you're facing? Tools such as **Cause & Effect Analysis**, the **5 Whys** Technique, and **CATWOE** are just some of the **problem-solving tools** that you'll need to be familiar with.

• Recognizing Opportunities: Do you **recognize opportunities** when they present themselves? Can you **spot a trend**? And are you able to create a plan to take advantage of the opportunities you identify?

Practical Skills

You also need the practical skills and knowledge needed to produce goods or services effectively, and run a company. You and any person that is on your staff as an employee must be equipped with skills to perform the services your business represents. Proper training and coaching the staff no matter how small or large to perform proper business etiquette is vital to the success and the performance of any business both small and large.

• Goal Setting: Do you regularly set **goals**, create a plan to achieve them, and then carry out that plan?
Planning and Organizing: Do you have the

talents, skills, and abilities necessary to achieve your goals? Can you coordinate people to achieve these efficiently and effectively? (Here, effective **project management skills** are important, as are basic **organization skills**.) And do you know how to develop a coherent, well thought-through **business plan**, including developing and learning from appropriate **financial forecasts**?

• Decision Making: **How good are you at making decisions?** Do you make them based on relevant information and by weighing the potential consequences? And are you confident in the decisions that you make?
Core decision-making tools include **Decision Tree Analysis**, **Grid Analysis**, and **Six Thinking Hats**.

You need knowledge in several areas when starting or running a business. For instance:

• Business knowledge: Do you have a good general knowledge of the main functional areas of a business (sales, marketing, finance, and operations), and are you able to operate or manage others in these areas with a reasonable degree of competence?
Entrepreneurial knowledge: Do you understand how entrepreneurs raise capital? And do you understand the sheer amount of

experimentation and hard work that may be needed to find a business model that works for you?

• Opportunity-specific knowledge: Do you understand the market you're attempting to enter, and do you know what you need to do to bring your product or service to market? Venture-specific knowledge: Do you know what you need to do to make this type of business successful? And do you understand the specifics of the business that you want to start? (This is where it's often useful to work for a short time in a similar business.)

You can also learn from others who have worked on projects similar to the ones that you're contemplating, or **find a mentor** – someone else who's been there before and is willing to coach you.

Is Running a Business for You?

Many entrepreneurs run into running a business head first. Most of the times not counting up the cost. Most businesses fail within the first year to five years of the business existence. Some people fail to plan, fail to know the vital skills or resources needed and some fail to properly manage or educate themselves with the tools needed to assure success. With this book and this particular chapter you are now armed with the tools, blueprint that you would need to carry out a successful business. Do you think you have what it takes?

Take a moment to make an analysis for your skills. You may be able to make it without a few of the skills listed or mentioned but the more you find yourself missing skills listed the less your chances are at achieving success with your business, let me be the voice of reason to tell you, you will fail. This analysis may lead you to understand that you many need to wait on starting your business to further your education and build your skill. Or you may altogether decide that entrepreneurship is not for you. Whatever choice you make be sure that it feels right. Running a business isn't for everyone.

The Newborn Entrepreneur

First Steps to Entrepreneurship

Chapter Four:

Identifying Your Interest and Abilities

1.   List your areas of interest. What are the things you are most passionate about? What are your hobbies? What would you like to learn? Take time to think about if pursuing business is something for you. The chances of your success will be greater when you love what you do and you are passionate about it.

2.   Write down your talents. Make the list extensive as possible; include abilities you wouldn't normally list on a resume. Such as expertise in public speaking, cooking, fishing, coin collecting, and child care are all examples of talents entrepreneurs have transformed into business.

3.   Note your personality strengths and weaknesses. Be honest, and get additional opinions from truthful people who you know well such as family, business associates, co-workers and friends. In order to develop into a

successful entrepreneur it is imperative that you know your strengths and weaknesses.

4.   Challenge yourself to find opportunities Evaluate your list for business potential. What type of business could you develop out of your skills, talents and interests or how about your expertise?

5.   Understand there's no such thing as a dumb idea. You need to spend time writing down your ideas, no matter how unusual they may appear to be. Use your imagination to its full potential. Even an outrageous thought may eventually lead to a feasible business plan.

6.   Develop an entrepreneur mindset. You have to begin to start thinking like an entrepreneur. What correlation can you make between your talents and existing business in your area? What gaps in their products or services could you fill? What problems can you solve that no one else has yet to think of?

7.   Take time to brainstorm with others to gain additional insight. Discuss your ideas with people who possess "the entrepreneurial mindset". Get your friends and family on any input the may have to help you improve or

validate your ideas. Feedback from friends and family can help you target and hone in on your ideas.

8. Seek mentoring from successful entrepreneurs; find entrepreneurs with thriving businesses and companies that will be willing to mentor emerging entrepreneurs. Focus on small companies; small business owners are typically entrepreneurs themselves. They are easier to contact and more willing to share information that owners of large companies.

9. Study the businesses you research. You can learn from the success and failures of others on your journey to becoming an entrepreneur. Visit their websites and physical locations. Study their ads and sample their products and services. What are they doing right or wrong? What areas of their business maybe lacking attention? What could you improve?

10. Contact a business owner. Explain your interest in their field and request a brief meeting at their convenience. If you happened to get turned down don't get discouraged, move on to the next possible prospect. Learn to be persistent and soon enough you will find

someone who is willing to share their expertise and knowledge.

11.   Prepare your questions before meeting you mentor or business owner. Preparing your questions before the meeting will allow you to get the bulk of the questions and information you most need answered. It will also allow you to manage your time as well as theirs. While meeting with this person consider this person a teacher who can help you think like an entrepreneur. Organize your questions in order of importance so you can remain on course as well as respect their time and schedule. If they express they are willing to meet with you again, accept the opportunity. Remember that having a mentor can help you navigate unfamiliar territory as you develop the characteristics of an entrepreneur.

I Hope You Fail!

Chapter Five:

"Losers quit when they fail. Winners fail until they succeed."

– Robert Kiyosaki

I know the heading of this chapter may come off a bit strong but I have my reasons. There's something about the threat of failure that becomes a turn on for the entrepreneur. While we all know that success is out there you will be greeted with countless encounters with failure before you shake hands or embrace success. One of the greatest teachers on success in the entrepreneur's life is not their college degree or how many books they read. They may not find the lessons to success in the mouth of their favorite celebrities, high paid entrepreneurs but may find it in FAILURE!

The one thing people set out to avoid is the very thing that makes us stronger. Without the lesson of failure many of us would not have developed the winning attitude that we have. For many minority entrepreneurs poverty was actually a gift in disguise that awakened their potential and frustrated them into producing a greater purpose. The fastest way to build a successful business from scratch is to fail fast.

Now you can take this road literally or you can embrace wisdom from those who set out on the journey to be successful and failed. Connecting yourself with mentors in your career path or those who succeeded in your field of passion will ignite you creative flow and momentum for success. Not because of all of their wonderful inspirational stories about how they made it to the top. Most real successful business owners and entrepreneurs who are given the opportunity will gladly tell you how they failed and how the road to realizing their dream was never easy. That's the story that's worth hearing vs. the how easy life is now version. We all know that money has the power to influence and opens doors for new opportunity, learn from the mistakes people made along the way so you can identify pitfalls and character flaws you may have and quickly rid yourself of them.

Nobody wants to fail; neither do they want to

be associated with failure and maybe that's why most people never start a business or probably build a successful business. Whichever side of the reason you rest on it's the same fear that motivates you to succeed or paralyzes you with failure; Isn't it interesting that it's the same fear that can make you achieve greatness and the same fear that can you avoid it? Some people never start a business because their mindset is messed up. They believe in their mind they are already going to fail before they start, and even if they do they wind up right.

The person, who greets failure but has a definite vision, will look failure in the face and say, "hello failure, I've seen you before but standing somewhere behind you is my success, can you please move". In fact people that are born with what I like to call the entrepreneur trait are blind to failure. They may count failure as lessons but they innately know that they can have what they envision and they will not stop until they attain it.

"Success is a poor teacher. We learn the most about ourselves when we fail, so don't be afraid of failing. Failing is part of the process of success. You cannot have success without failure." – Rich Dad

The Newborn Entrepreneur

In order to build a successful business you have to be willing to confront failure. Everyone is ready to succeed but few are really willing to endure its process. Success is like a high maintenance woman; it will court you and date you until you are rich enough and wise enough to marry it. While you're on your road to a successful business you may be introduced to failure and if you do meet failure pick it up as a lesson and move on. I have never met a successful entrepreneur who has not had a share of failure.

Let me share two deeply intelligent people who failed before they succeeded. Their example is empowering to any entrepreneur looking to gain success:

Example 1: Thomas Edison failed 10,000 times before he invented the incandescent bulb and this is what he has to say; "*I **have not failed. I have just found 10,000 ways that won't work.***" – Thomas Edison

This quote from Thomas Edison revolutionized my way I looked at leadership, entrepreneurship and the creative arts. So many people give up when they mishap or fail. Your failure just maybe a way of doing something that Just doesn't work. I've been known to say over and over again, "failure is redirection". When I see failure, I know it's an opportunity to go back to the drawing board and come up with a new plan.

Example 2: Henry Ford had two business failures and with the experience gathered from those business failures, he went on to build **Ford Motor Company** and became one of the richest men in history. "*Failure is just a resting place. It is an opportunity to begin again more intelligently.*" – Henry Ford

I don't know about you, but if you could even envision failure as a pit stop so that you can rest, build your strength up again and go back out into battle. Let me remix Henry Ford's statement by saying it like this, *"Failure is opportunity to begin again more intelligently".* Failure though it baffles the mind, it brings out a more excellent you, failure births new intelligence. Your mind will being surfacing a new brilliance that you have never brought out before.

> "*I can accept failure, everyone fails at something. But I cannot accept not trying.*" – Michael Jordan

Despite my massive failures, the experienced gathered from these failures is priceless. You'll never know what works and what doesn't if you don't fail; you will never know your limitation and capabilities until you risk failing.

Do I look at myself today and think I am a failure? No! I don't think so, not in the least! I might not have accomplished all that I've wanted to do yet but I am still in the Entrepreneur race! I have not quit yet, In fact I think I am just getting started. No doubt you can pick your life up, dust yourself off and count your "failures as life lessons and stepping stones for the road in which you're heading.

Overnight Success

Chapter Six:

"In the game of entrepreneurship, the process is more important than the goal. When you start building a business, you begin a journey, a process. This process has a beginning and an ending and between the beginning and end lays a lot of challenges. You will win only if you remain faithful to the process." - Rich Dad

We have all heard of the term "overnight success", for some people it sounds good to them and to others it puts a bad taste in their mouth. How many of us dream of starting a business or company and immediately striking it rich. When you're in that state of mind you tend to day dream about what some call "the good life". In case I am not clear on what "the good life" is the definition really varies with us all. Just like we all have our own separate DNA and no one else on this earth carries your DNA but you, we all have a dream or desire inside of us that seems to be our own. No matter how many people are out there trying to do what you want to do, you still see your vision different from others.

The one tale we have to stop telling ourselves is the dream of "overnight success". It sounds good to the ears, it's what you want to hear, it might even be who you want to be, but you must let that dream die. Aiming for overnight success is like playing the lotto, "it's a one in a million chance". Trying to make a name overnight is the one idea worth letting go of. Now that does not mean for some it doesn't come. If it comes let it come, but guess what? It appears that it happened overnight but the truth of the matter is it took hours of study, hours of research, and hours of preparation, planning and investing here and there when you could. Then finally your efforts start to pay off!

"*A short cut is the longest distance between two points.*"

– Anonymous

If I could tell you the truth about shortcuts my personal opinion would be that short cuts are like building a business in midair. It may go up fast but without a proper foundation it my plummet into disaster. So taking the time to build a business and your entrepreneurial pursuit right from the start, it paces you and allows you to ride the current with a flow. You're in the driver's seat and you can control where you're going. You can stop or speed up; the power is in your hands.

Everyone wants to be the next Oprah, Tyler Perry, Les Brown, T.D. Jakes, Cindy Trimm, Bill Gates, Larry Ellison or Mark Zuckerberg. If I could tell the truth myself I've never wanted to be these people, but I have been guilty of desiring their financial affluence and influence into the lives of people. The truth of the matter is no matter what success I build and achieve in my own life I should never desire what someone else has. The truth is they paid for the place that there in and that's what qualifies them to be who they are and where they are. Now people may look at your life and wish they had you skill, influence, speaking ability, wit or charisma.

Trying make yourself like someone else is not wise. Comparing yourself and measuring yourself to someone else is not wise. God doesn't even do that! Ask me how I know? Because he knows every hair on your head, he fearfully and wonderfully made you; no one has your DNA and finger print. He's thought about you so well that there's not one person on earth like you. While we may have similarities God made us all unique. Everyone is trying to get in alignment with the who's who, but who told you that this is the way to go? You're trying to line up when God wants you to stand out! Instead of blending in, blend out. Stand out, be daring, be bold and be different! If you're ever going to be successful in business and entrepreneurship you have to "do it like you do it". Don't try to be like anyone else. The world will reward your difference, not your similarity!

The one common truth about Oprah, Tyler Perry, Les Brown, T.D. Jakes, Cindy Trimm, Bill Gates, Larry Ellison or Mark Zuckerberg is that people admire their wealth and affluence but they don't want their process. All of these people faced some hardships that helped mold them into the person that they are. If you want what they have then you also want every trial and battle that it took to make them who they are. Then you want their depression, poverty, molestation, mental challenges and any other failure that can be named. People seem to come in on the intermission of your story and see all the wonders but they don't know the beginnings and "the makings of you" that brought you to your present place.

"The height attained by great men is not by sudden flight. For while their companions lay asleep, these men were toiling in the night."

– Anonymous

All Business beginning from the planning phase before proceeding into the startup phase; how many times have we heard the expression "when you fail to plan you plan to fail". While most of the time we frown on these expressions how true do they become to us. Were so busy looking down on people for using these statements because they are over used at times and they start to lose their strength and value. I don't know about you but I don't have time to fail, that's why before making moves I have to know the success it could lead to and more importantly the failures that can come from it. After counting up all the cost I make my move, whatever lot I end up at is well with me because I did my part.

People look at these companies and CEO's who have made it big and forget that even though they may be a rising and high performing business before they came into the public eye they were somewhere in the back of the line getting there start. No one starts out on top. You have to work your way up and earn it honestly. You can ask any CEO who has started a company and they will tell you people look at your present success and measure you and judge you by it, not knowing it may have taken you 1000 failed attempts and finally one successful strike that made a difference and what took 1001 attempts played out over 10 years. So maybe it wasn't 10 years and 1001 attempts. Maybe you started 3 failed businesses but the 4th one prospered. Most people don't ask about the failures they only talk about the success they see.

*"**Most people say the Rich Dad Company is an overnight success and I admit, we are an overnight success but it took us ten years to get there.***" – Robert Kiyosaki

Success is a process, there's no fast ticket to it. We have to ditch the "overnight success syndrome". We also have to get rid of the "get rich quick mindset". Holding on to these fictitious mindsets can be poisonous to the channeling of our entrepreneurial success. One of the key things is learning how to pace yourself and endure the process you must go through to build your achievements. You will get there, you should never rush the process you might leave out some important details or wind up running into unexpected pitfalls. Learn all you can while you're still in your process, it will help you stay on top when you do arrive there and be able to remain profitable and successful.

All successful entrepreneurs went through a process to get to their present status. While things seem to pay off quickly for some it was a process for others. No matter the process, you must stick to the plan! Now I can't tell **how long it will take you to complete your own process** and you will never know because you don't have a crystal ball to foresee the future. All I can tell you is that **everybody's entrepreneurial path is different**. It's up to you to find yours and you will never find it except you start the entrepreneurial process. While you're on your journey remember to keep loving what you do, it will make your work seem less of a chore or job and be a more rewarding process.

The Newborn Entrepreneur

The Time Is Now

Chapter Seven:

"My best advice to an entrepreneur is this, "there's no such thing as a dumb idea". - Michael McCain

Could it be possible that you're sitting on a million dollar business right now? Could it be very well possible that you have a million dollar dream but your still sleep? It's time to awaken the millionaire in you. (If you reading this I also recommend that you read my book "The Millionaire Class"). Do you remember when your grandparents and parents told you that a dollar is not what it used to be? Did you think they were just being funny penny pinchers? It hasn't been until recent years that peoples view on money has drastically changed and people are taking money more serious. People want to know how to make more money, save more money and get out of debt!

If you're anything like me, I know I have an affluent mind. Let me describe it like this, "I am a genius learning how to control my mind". I am good at coming up with money making ideas and plans. Yet there's a part of me that will build up an idea in its greatest form, I do all the research and count up the cost. Then my evil twin comes along (my Gemini nature) and destroys the idea. Better spoken, it's those self-defeating sabotaging thoughts that come along to give you every reason why you can't do something. (For more of my points of views with handling self-sabotage get my book "Life Editing Vol. I).

The problem every neonate entrepreneur has to face is making sure that their idea is profitable. Once you begin counting up the cost you will know if your idea gets the green light for go, or should you press your breaks and look for the closest rest point for a new idea. I know plenty of people who could be making a substantial income with a side business or entrepreneurial pursuit but they lock themselves out by discrediting ideas that come to them. Think of your ideas as angles that God sends to you on an assignment to bring you a gift. Now after the idea comes to you it's up to you to do what it necessary to make that idea come to pass. Here are some of my power tips for manifestation:

1.   *Write your ideas down* Remember that it's not enough to just write down your thought's but you must make plain what you are seeing and envisioning. No one knows what you're seeing but you. So when you are a visionary you have to learn the art of communicating your vision clearly.

2.   *Research* – When entering into any business no matter how big or small you need to know your market (demographic) and the estimated cost for the business you plan to start.

3.   *Set Goals* Start setting goals for things you need to achieve to get the business started. (Incorporation, licenses, permits, copy rights, business plans etc. maybe some of the things on your list to do).

4.   *Find an Advisor* Find someone who has done what you're looking to do. Offer them lunch or dinner where you can sit and talk about what you want to do with your business. Make sure you take notes and glean from their advice, after all you either just paid for it or you paid for the lunch or dinner so get your monies worth and your worth of time.

5.   *Keep a positive attitude* We have all heard the expression that "attitude determines your altitude". Well in my opinion it's the truth!

Entrepreneurship is already a challenging task, why make it any harder than what it needs to be? Keep a success driven mindset and you should be on your way to greatness.

6.   *Stick to the plan* Once you have a plan in place to get your business started, as long as it is not a faulty plan full of errors and pitfalls stick to it! Stick to the plan and run the course until you reach your goals and achieve them. Don't get in mid-gear and decide to star revising things you will only get confuse or forfeit the success that could have been made.

If we really tell the truth to ourselves "there will never be a perfect time to start a business". If you're waiting for a green light that say's "go" you may never see it! If you apply the manifestation steps that I gave you above I'm sure that you will tackle staring your new business with ease. The next tip I'll give you a heads up on is that you have to "ditch trying to be a perfectionist". If you sit around trying to perfect every angle of what you're doing you will waste time and energy. There's a clear difference from being a perfectionist and walking in excellence! When you have the spirit of excellence you know what you do you do well. You also are confident that you are performing at your best. You are making significant landmarks that are leading you to complete goals. This is the type of attitude and brilliance you need as an entrepreneur.

"I am an entrepreneur in hot pursuit of my destiny" – Michael McCain

There are 3 keys to becoming an entrepreneur with multi-million dollar potential and those 3 keys are:

1. *The Right Plan* - Let s start with the right pan, I described a little of the process of this in my power tips to manifestation earlier in this chapter. Yet I can't begin to stress it enough that a plan is the very starting point for it all. When you have a business, whether working for yourself as an entrepreneur or creating a business that employ's others you have to be on you "A game". You have to make clear as a visionary the going plan for your business and know where you plan to end up.

There are plenty of people who set out to start a business and fail in their attempt because they don't know what they are doing, how they plan to get to their goals. Last but definitely not least they also can't get the appropriate help or funding because people don't know how to help them. This is why making a business plan, purpose statement or mission statement an important part of what needs to be done. This makes clear what you set out to do. Bankers, investors or lenders want to know where you stand. Can you pay back the money or is this a "favor" they can write off. Again the power is in your hands to be able to communicate effectively your vision.

2.   *The Right Team* – Every entrepreneur needs a team. This team may be made up of the most skilled employees of contracted workers you can find, or it may be down to personal friends and love ones who pitch in help, but you can't do it all by yourself. Everyone needs help and no man is an island when it comes to entrepreneurial success.

Needless to say that you should be connecting and partnering with people who believe in what you do, people that understand your goals, people that have the skill to help you get there. I would advise to ditch anyone who you have to keep pulling along the way, they are nothing but dead weight, they will be a major hindrance to your flow, success, and your business.

3.   *The Money*- Last but not least you need the money right? Duh... You need money to get your business off the ground so how do you plan to do it? Most entrepreneurs don't have a dime at hand to get their companies started. I love entrepreneurship when it comes from people who start from scratch and had nothing. I love watching the success stories and learning how people made it. That success story could be you. Now all you have do is plan

how you will bring in the money to make it all work. Finding investors, having parties or selling dinners where people can invest in your vision are all ideas people have used to fund their companies. Wouldn't it be great to have a dinner party centered on your business plan and allow close friends and family the opportunity to donate to your cause? (Countless entrepreneurs have used this strategy and it works!)

Start Playing the Game

Just in case I have not made myself abundantly clear "there will never a perfect time to start a business!" I have allot of friends who are enthusiastic about starting a business; some of them share their plans with me and I have to admit there are times I walk away frustrated with myself because I sat around wasting time and not doing what I should be doing to make my plans come to pass. There were a few things I learned about myself:

1. Was that I needed to change my friends, because I was surrounded by people who just "talk about where they are going and what they plan to do and never do anything!"

2. "The do nothing spirit" was on me. I had to ditch procrastination, ditch the sluggards and hang around people motivated to achieve

greatness. When that happens, you will start realizing your dreams!

Now getting back to my sluggard friends, I would hear stuff like "Dr. Mike, I'm waiting for the right time to start. I can't afford to make a wrong move; I really can't afford any mistakes."

My answer would be this: You know there will never be what we think is the right time to start a business. When you say "you can't afford to make a wrong move" I say you already are in debt by the move you made. You already have loss without moving. When you say "I really can't afford any mistakes" my answer is the mistake has already been made and each day that you go by unfulfilling your dream you're paying a high price ticket. That doesn't mean you just jump up start a business at random but when you have walked out your power steps to manifestation and you have a solid plan in place, what are you waiting for?

"*The way to get started is to quit talking and begin doing*."

– Walt Disney

As a neonate entrepreneur you have to get out of the starting position. You can't sit in the race stall forever! You have to get out and get into the game. Sometimes fear of losing gives you anxieties about starting before you can put your first foot forward. Ditch those worries and find your motivation. You have to get the plan in place, now stick to the plan and work the game! Defeat is not an option for you, procrastination is not an option either, get your-self-motivated and the wheels of your success running toward achievement.

"You have to act and act now."

– Larry Ellison

As Time Goes On

We all know time stops for no man, when I see some of those same friends a few months later, a few years later they never started their dream business. Year after year still in the same dead end job or career that they were in. As an entrepreneur I had an extreme wakeup call around my 24th birthday. I was reading a young entrepreneurs article and the writer was talking about young millionaires and starting a business and making millions in success. I am sitting there reading the article and with every story I read about these young millionaires I started laughing saying "that's me, that's me". Before long I arrived to a line that forever changed my life!

"Young entrepreneurs need to know if you don't start young with your dreams, chances are when you reach the age of 26-27 years old those dreams will die!"

What! As I sat there, my eyes engulfed with tears and I said to myself I am 2 years away from dying? (Not literally, but at least the thought of it motivated me enough to start doing something). While I knew I was not going to die a physical death, the words I read shook me enough to get up off my derriere and start dusting off old dreams, business plans and ideas. Made a few phone calls that would set me on my way, I called some close friends and made them accountability partners. I asked them to be my accountability partners that will make sure I am not giving up on my work.

Well it worked! Before long I had connected with a few people and partnered to start my new business. After all I was not a business virgin I had a few partners in business before and knew how to play the game. I went head on into my plans to start my business with no protection! I knew it was my plan this time to conceive. I had flirt around with my ideas but never got in bed with no one to make these plans come to pass. (Of course you know I don't mean sleeping around in the literal form, but I mean lying my ideas down with someone that I trust enough to help me through gestation into birthing).

As time went on I killed the feeling of waiting on the right time. I motivated myself to take all the steps necessary that I had so carefully outlined and revised over and over again; Thinking that I only had 24 months to live (2 years) was enough time to get me to make something happen to get me on the road to my dreams being manifested. When I think about the progress made during this time I know that by a long shot I am nowhere near finished, the journey is just getting started.

The truth about entrepreneurship is that it's all about risk taking; calculated risk to be precise. Not the random risk taking that some people perform not counting up the cost that lies ahead. It's the risk involved that makes starting a business or building a business an exciting task. The thrill of successfully building a business from scratch makes the experience worthwhile and rewarding. You don't need to have every single detailed thing in place when you start a business; start with what you have and you will pick the rest up along the way.

"Risk — if one has to jump a stream and knows how wide it is, he will not jump. If he doesn't know how wide it is, he'll jump and six times out of ten, he'll make it." – *Anonymous*

Amazon was started in the garage by Jeff Bezos; so was the Ford Motor Corporation. Facebook, Google, Yahoo and Dell computers were started in the dorm of various schools. The entrepreneurs behind these companies had great business ideas but had no capital and business team. But did lack of startup capital and a business team stop these men? The answer is no. If these men hadn't started; they wouldn't have been approached by partners, investors and Venture Capitalists. Are you ready to take your business idea to the market? Get on the road to creating your business and you can be named one of the entrepreneur success stories we will soon see on the news. People are waiting for you product, for your invention, for your record label, song, music site, book, talk show, cookbook or any other creative venture you may think of or come up with.

> **"Begin to weave and God will give the thread." – Anonymous**

> **"In today's rapidly changing world, the people who are not taking risk are the risk takers.**" – Robert Kiyosaki

When I first started out as an entrepreneur I was completely helpless. Left to the mercy of every book I could read and the internet to guide my way. When I speak to most people about entrepreneurship they always state "you're so knowledgeable about things it's hard to believe you didn't go to school for this" the only schooling I had for entrepreneurship was starting 2 businesses in my early teens, one of them landing me to work for a millionaire preacher in New York. The other was successfully running several non-profit organizations which helped me to build my public speaking ability and teaching skills. I developed natural leadership skills and communication skills which paid off and took me to the present place of where I am.

The Newborn Entrepreneur

Today I work with a conglomerate of companies; I sit as president and CEO of several companies. I am a life coach and consultant to many high impact entrepreneurs across the country. I can't believe some of the achievements I made for my age. I could have never come this far holding on to fear, fear will paralyze you and cause you to become immobile. When you get a plan and a vision, you have to set your face like flint and go for the target goal. You also have to understand that people that start out with you might not end with you, you can never base your work around friendships, partnerships with people because when it comes to business those are ever changing factors.

As an entrepreneur you have to start building somewhere. You can't keep looking at your business plan and never acting on it. What good is a success journal or idea journal when none of the ideas in its contents have been worked on or brought into manifestation? When you put your best foot forward the rest will start to flow. People who take no risk are taking the biggest risk of all, "the risk of do nothing". Do nothing but full of ideas and creativity leads to poverty. You have to get up and produce something!

The Spirit of Expectation

Chapter Eight:

"Preparation is the father of all expectation." – Michael McCain

Preparing for the best is important; expecting the worst is most important. I have always been one to say nothing catches me by surprise. Surprise is an element that I have suspended out of my life because sometimes I think things out so well I can predict what the failure outcome would be, the risk I am taking, and I am good at counting up the cost. One law of success that I taught myself was whatever goal I am aiming to reach always aim above that goal because chances are ill hit it dead on target or fall below it.

Hence my personal law of success to those who don't understand my method I always seem to have standards that are too high or goals that seem to be outlandish. I have to aim as high as possible because I personally don't like the feeling of "almost". I don't want "almost" make it, I desire to reach my goals or exceed them. You can always make that accomplishment when you push yourself to raise your standards. Raise your target goal, prepare for bad times and know that you will always need something to fall back on.

> *"Prepare for bad times and you will only know good times."*
>
> – Robert Kiyosaki

As humans, it's normal to pray and always expect good times. Even in school, we were instructed to always prepare for the best but never did we hear anyone mention we should expect the worst. When we know that bad times are evitable it lessens the effect and the power failure can have over you. Some people sacrifice everything they have taking a gamble with business hoping to make it. Sometimes never counting up the cost and its effects; I am not talking about that type of failure. I am talking about when you know you have done everything right but fate never allowed you plan to work out.

> *"Smooth seas do not make skillful sailors."* – Anonymous

As an entrepreneur and business owner, **I can confidently tell you that the business world is filled with bed of roses but you have to go through the thorns to get to the bed of roses.** You may find yourself cut by the thorns a few times but eventually you will get to the beauty of the rose. Business ideas are interesting to behold on paper; building a business is exciting in the planning phase because of its future prospects. But the reality of starting a business manifests the moment that business is launched; and this reality is the major reason why most entrepreneurs give up after the failure of their first business startup. They wish they never started the process and they vow never to repeat it. At this stage, the more determined entrepreneur dust themselves off; bandage up any cuts from the thorns and gets back in the field looking for the beauty of the roses.

*"**Preparing for the best is important; expecting the worst is most important & Preparation is the father of all expectation"***

Michael McCain

To successfully **start a business and navigate the harsh business terrain**, you have to be adequately prepared but most importantly, **you must also expect the worst**. Now when I say expect the worst I am not talking about in a worrisome stressful way. Just know that there are risks involve or chances for failure. Never expect a 100 % increase on your investment. While I will admit that if it were all possible for such an opportunity we would first all be taking it and second we would all be rich!

 When I am approached by budding neonate entrepreneurs who are over enthusiastic about their self-proclaimed "**fool-proof business idea**," I politely remind them about **the 50-50 probability of success and failure.** No matter your level of success, the odds will still be there. There's no such business that you can go in that rewards you with a 100% return and no loss profits. No matter what business you enter into they all have failure potential.

"Business, more than any other occupation, is a continual calculation, an instinctive exercise in foresight."

– Henry R. Luce

The ultimate reason **I advocate you expect the worst is because when you expect the worst and prepare towards it, the worst will never happen.** You may **go bankrupt or lose your investment capital**. To the outside world, you are finished but deep down inside you were prepared; you know it's not the worst. Why? The reason is because **you expected and prepared towards it. Donald Trump has gone bankrupt twice but he roared back after each bankruptcy because it wasn't the worst situation for him.**

Building a business is not like having a job, where you can predict your time of promotion and expected pay. In business, you must thrive on uncertainty. Employees expect the best, entrepreneurs expect the worst and when the worst finally come to entrepreneurs, it won't be the worst. Remember my personal law of success, always aim higher than your expected target. You will either hit the target or land right below it, the choice is yours. It's all in your preparation. Coach yourself through it, you have to tell yourself, "your worst looks good on you because greater and better is coming". You have to fail sometimes as the motivational tool necessary to push you into greater accomplishments.

Now how do you prepare for the worst? I definitely don't have the answer to that question because I can't teach you how to expect and prepare for the worst. But a great way to start is by having a contingency plan; or better still, an exit strategy or plan B. The only successful plan for hard times is having a contingency plan. Setting up a contingency fund for yourself and your business will allow you to have cash to fall back on when business gets slow or all together nonexistent. It will give you the empowerment you need to continue or strategize another plan or avenue of escape.

*"**Always start at the end before you begin. Professional investors always have an exit strategy before they invest. Knowing your exit strategy is an important investment fundamental.**" – Rich Dad*

Before I go into any business, I prepare and plan for the best; after which I prepare for the worst by putting a contingency plan in place. A contingency plan is always my landing haven should I eventually get hit by the worst. It's the sole reason why I still have the audacity to start new businesses even after a business failure. I know the law of probability and I know the law of risk. The same way I get a plan to succeed, a plan that I absolutely believe in, I also plan a   safe place to fall should my plan fail me.

When you adequately plan your future you count up the possible failures.
You also take the appropriate time to envision the end from the beginning. Be it success or failure I've thought about them all, I teach myself how to become a master mind at strategy. I learn when to move and when not to move. I learn when to play and when the game is over. That is the success of expectation. Taking control over your outcome and envisioning the end from the beginning.

The Newborn Entrepreneur

Stop Tripping Over Yourself

Chapter Nine:

Successful at nothing, don't we all know some people who fall into that category. They are always busy doing something but never seem to be making any significant or meaningful strides at anything. You ever met someone who is just absolutely clumsy they trip over themselves while walking. That's what some entrepreneurs are like. They are like the clumsy friend or relative we all have who seems to fail at putting one step in front of the other.

Your success or failure in business are all hinged on one important factor; you! There's no one to blame for your success or failure. You have to take full responsibility. It's our human proclivity to want to avoid taking the blame for things and finding someone else to put at fault for our mishaps. Yet the flip side of our human behavior is to take credit for any good that comes out of something. Be it your success or your failure you're fully responsible.

*"**The biggest challenge you have is to challenge your own self-doubt and your laziness. It is yourself doubt and your laziness that defines and limit who you are.**"* – Rich Dad

Another make or breaker factor for the neonate entrepreneur is learning "the power of your mindset". Everything to succeed might be in place but **if you are not prepared, if you are not in the right mindset; you will fail even when presented with a perfect idea and business team**. One of the golden keys to success is learning how to work your mind and not you're behind! You have to work on the art of strategy and planning. Your mindset is the key to the measure of success or failure you attribute.

*"**Getting rich begins with the right mindset, the right words and the right plan.**"* – Rich Dad

Being in the right entrepreneurial mindset means **being prepared to fail; it means being prepared to go beyond your comfort zone and finally, it means being prepared to give your business everything it requires to make it a success**. Being in the right mindset means **being prepared to hold on to your dreams** even in the face of criticism. People give criticism to what they don't understand and what they can't control. One thing I learned about being a visionary is not everyone see what you see. Make clear what your vision is. It will not only help you but it will help people who connect with you.

"The size of your success is measured by the strength of your desire, the size of your dream and how you handle disappointment along the way."

– Rich Dad

When I start thinking about all of my past experience, I can confidently tell you that starting a business and building a business from scratch is indeed a sacrifice. Sometime you will experience losses that cause you pain. As the saying goes, no pain no gain. It's the pain you experience early on sometimes that a book could never teach you. Yet you learn from those experiences and start building the next strategy for success. Truly that is exactly what the process of building a business is, finding the right strategy!

It's nearly needless to say that upon building a business it will require moments and times of sacrifice. A time will come when you will need to dedicate longer hours to your work. Sometimes you'll be pulling 60-80 hours per week just to see your business get through the small business startup phase. Those tender early days of your business come with sleepless nights, emotional stress and mind bending challenges. There will be plenty of times where things seem to be stacked against you and nothing going according to your plan or as you desired. You will start to have an overwhelming compulsive feeling of giving up. Now why would you make it this far to give up now? Tread a little further and see what your end will be.

Ultimately you have to keep in mind what your goals are, what's your purpose. There will be times you will have to stamp your vision statement on your chest and march forward like a solider out to battle and trust that all opposing forces will be rendered powerless. You are wise enough and strong enough to win; remember what your vision is and march forward to it until it is accomplished no matter the odds you may face. As a matter of fact who told you accomplishing your vision was going to be easy anyway? There's a saying that says "anything worth having is worth fighting for". Do you believe that? Then fight for your vision and for your success, it's already yours!

*"**You can always quit so why quit now.**"* – Rich Dad

When you change people change

The reason I can stand and offer this wisdom is because for years I have been a full time entrepreneur my entire life. I've never had to work for anyone and for years I have maintained and stride with the changes that I needed to make for my freedom and financial improvement. Each step that I made was worth everything I had to face. I can admit there were times I was going through things feeling like would any of it be worth it? As a time went on I discovered as I taped into my purpose I began to notice that my friends began to change. My friends started to represent more of what I loved and loved doing then just being people I grew up with or was associated with.

I quickly started learning that my old friends didn't represent where I was going and it wasn't because they were bad. It was simply because their gifts and callings were different. Things I was interested in doing they were not and it often put a strain on things. I had to learn to balance who I spend my time with and know what it's just going to be for fun and enjoyment. No inspiration may come out of this; no work will be the result of this but just quality time with people I love.

As my old friends changed I gained new ones. New friends started manifesting in my life that sometimes strikingly represented my same interest and concerns. They played the same game I played. They believed the same things I believed. They walked the same walk I walked. They talked the same talk I talked. Some were even wiser than I was and I was not intimidated by that, because I understood in order to be successful I cannot be the smartest person in the group. I needed people that had something I didn't have and besides that I love taking the back seat and learning to activate my purpose.

Considering the type of business you will be getting into it may cause a lifestyle shift. Not only will the work you do change, the setting, and the people surrounding you but your mindset as well. I had to give up my lifestyle and I had to automatically become humble because I knew nothing with respect to running a business the way some of my other counterparts did. Humility is key to opening yourself up to new knowledge. You need to be teachable. Because I was determined to make it I gave up allot of pleasures of life to take a new mindset to set me in the place I needed to be. I denied myself sometimes of sleep, spending time hanging out or going out to eat and be social as I often loved doing. I knew I had to make a few sacrifices and that it would be for a short time but it would pay off.

"I rest when I feel fulfilled"

- Dr. Michael McCain

When you're in entrepreneurship you quickly learn that sacrifice is one of the tests and proofs of if a business will make it or fold. Building a business from scratch often requires everything you've got. You have to be willing and tolerant to making sacrifices. Successful entrepreneurs such as Tyler Perry, Steven Jobs, Les Brown, Bill Gates and Mark Zuckerberg sacrificed their education to build the business of their dreams. Often times one of the sacrifices would be giving up job security. I am not asking you to do any of these; all I want you to grasp and understand that the power you have on the inside of you. The choices for where you will end up in your career or finances are literally in your hands. It's up to you to step out on the invisible and make it possible. It's up to you to do it. Entrepreneurship is a personal undertaking, you can't be force or persuaded into it. It has to ignite within you and you have to initiate the act of pursuit. Begin to ask yourself and meditate on whether you're ready to being the process?

The Philosophy of Entrepreneurship

True entrepreneurship is about standing and walking in your truth. For every entrepreneur the rules are different. As a matter of fact most entrepreneurs are infamous for creating their own rules that get them to their expected end. The mind of an entrepreneur is always thinking against the grain. Entrepreneurs usually do not participate in existing opportunities, but begin to bring new opportunities into existence.

"*Remain true to yourself and your philosophy.*"

-Giorgio Armani

The philosophy of entrepreneurship is birthed when an entrepreneur sets themselves in a place for rational investigation of the truths and principles of being such as it applies to their career or field; applying the knowledge or conduct necessary for success and achievement of their goals.

The philosophy of entrepreneurship breaks down in 3 important ways:

1.   Natural Philosophy: The study of practical knowledge and acquisition.

2.   Moral Philosophy: The personal alignment of lifestyle and ethics.

3.   Metaphysical Philosophy: The mental and spiritual discipline of aligning your consciousness, behavior and awareness.

The philosophy of entrepreneurship is the science of basic principles and concepts of a particular branch of knowledge, especially with a view to improving or reconstituting ethics, habits, knowledge and lifestyle. So in a nutshell the philosophy of entrepreneurship is a system of principles for guidance, discipline and lifestyle to the entrepreneur.

*"**Press on. Nothing in the world can take the place of persistence. Talent will not; nothing is more common than unsuccessful men with talent. Genius will not; the world is full of educated derelicts. Persistence and determination alone are omnipotent**."*

-Ray Kroc

The Newborn Entrepreneur

 If you're going to be successful as an entrepreneur you have to be witty. You cannot think you know it all. Entrepreneurship is a game that the more it changes the more things stay the same. There are some foundations of truth that everyone can benefit from, yet there are some changes that are inevitable that everyone one needs to prepare for. You have to stay in the press. You can't let your fire burnout; the true blood of an entrepreneur is persistence. Entrepreneurs don't take no for an answer because all their spirit hears is YES!

There are plenty of unsuccessful people in the world who constantly talk about what they plan to do and achieve nothing. Yet these same men and women are talented sometimes beyond understanding. The world is full of educated people which appear to be dumb because of their lack of ability to apply what they have learned. Dare to step out of your comfort zone to be, to do and become the person you know you are meant to be.

The Laws of Entrepreneurship I

Chapter Ten:

In my recent years I spent allot of time meditating on what success meant to me. Year after year I believe that my definition evolved, it didn't out right change. It was experiences and new knowledge that added to the depth of my definition. As a matter of fact, one of the highest contributors was my experiences with failure. It is common that when we battle with things we fail at we will start looking at our lives differently. During this mental battle with my failures and achievements in life I summed up what I felt the total of success meant to me, "success is the sum total of the consistency of purpose".

As a neonate entrepreneur you have to stay in line with things that mean something to you. Your diligence and consistency is the key to what defines and builds lasting success in your life. Not only will it build the success you are looking for but it will mold your character, skills and habits which are the other contributors to your success. Regardless of your definition of success, there are, oddly enough, a great number of common characteristics that are shared by successful business people. We will outline those characteristics in depth in this chapter so hang tight.

The Laws of Entrepreneurship are a set of laws that are promised to work for the person who is looking to become a fortune 500 company, to the person who is looking to start a local business or successful stay at home business. While this chapter is rich with tips and principles that you will want to live by and remember it is a chapter that really sounds like a book of its own.

1.   *Do what you enjoy, Do what you love*
One of the keys to a successful business is to do something you love doing. I've attended countless entrepreneurship summits and conferences to hear this truth over and over

again. At first I ignored it, but as time went on is started watching people go into business doing things for the sake of money and failing. I also saw people who began to be unhappy with their work. Entrepreneurship in my opinion has always been about doing what you love, you gain personal satisfaction from growing a business out of what you love. When you're doing what you love, no matter how fast or slow the business is growing you never lose the passion because it's something that you love. When you're in business only for the money you quickly start to lose interest and your focus fades and you begin looking for the next quick opportunity. When you don't enjoy what you're doing it is likely that it will begin to show in the success or failure of your business. The failure that some entrepreneur's face is the loss of passion while building their business. Sometimes that loss of passion comes by not counting up the cost, and not having resources and mentoring.

2. *Take what you do seriously—*

   Pursuing the road to becoming a successful entrepreneur you have to pull your expectations into alignment and focus on believing in your dream. In other words simply put, **you have to believe in yourself!** (That includes believing in whatever service product or goods you sell. Trust that you're performing at top quality and providing a quality product). You have to keep your foot to the grind stone and not become lax in your business dealings. Too many people that pursue home based entrepreneurship become lax and fall behind in sales or performance. When you begin to lax in performance you leave yourself open as a target. When people come along that don't believe in what you're doing you will be easily moved or discouraged because your performance is out of alignment.

There are people who don't believe you're a business owner if you don't have an office or perform your work out of such as an office building, store front and etc. Little do people know home based entrepreneurs make good money and it is an industry that has grown by leaps and bounds in recent years.

3. *Plan Everything*

No matter if you have a home based business, store front, factory or office building, you have to take what you do seriously and make it a matter of such importance that it requires a plan. You need to develop a plan that you can implement and maintain. Business planning is no joke, it's so important because it requires you to analyze each business situation, do your research and put together all your data.

Business planning is practically your second step. It's a well thought out plan as to how your business will operate and work. I learned the importance of this as I began to grow as an entrepreneur because I found myself having a big and vast vision needing to learn how to trust people to help me fulfill the vision of my business. I also had to learn how to identify people who would be suitable to work with my vision or serve it. Having a business plan allowed me to be able to employ the right people as well as give them a guide to follow as to how our system works.

Business planning allows you to measure the success and failures of your business. How well you're doing and where you may be failing at. Sometimes your plans can be edited or change, improved to what works for you or what works for the business more importantly.

4.   *Manage Your Money*- The pulse that sets the tone for the thriving business is cash

flow. You need money to run and operate your business no matter how large or small your business is. You need to buy inventory, pay for services, promote and market your business, repair or replace equipment and pay yourself (or employees) so that you can continue your work.

So everyone from the small business owner to the million dollar entrepreneur needs to become wise in their affairs with handling money. You need to be financially wise with money to ensure that cash keeps flowing in. To be sure that your business is growing in profits and not just surviving. When you first start a business it will take a while before you see a significant profit. Yet you have to maintain your work and your finances and stay away from any gray areas or the invisible red line.

Money Management outlines:

A.   The money you receive from clients in exchange for your goods and services you provide.
        (Income)
B.   The Money you spend on inventory, supplies, wages and other items required to keep your business operating.

(Expenses)

C.   The Books: keeping honest and correct books to show expenses and payouts for management purposes and tax payer information.

5.   *The Art of Sales* –Any entrepreneur in business needs to grow the skill of making a sale; from the product, to the service and building returning clientele. The fact that I have found is when you do what you do well the word will spread and word of mouth brings you better business than paying top dollars for advertising. As a matter of fact, advertising usually just makes your company's image look big but leads to very little sales. If you really want to make a sale you have to do it the old fashion way and be knowledgeable, personable and genuine and **just ask for the sale**! That does not mean that advertising, marketing, branding and other useful tools are a complete waste. It just leads to very few sales. Just remember to be genuine and forward (not demanding) and ask for the sale.

6.   *Know Your Customers*– When you're in business you have to know your demographic which is your client base and market; you also have to remember to make your clients a

matter of importance. Sometimes entrepreneurs can be guilty of venturing off into finding their own pleasures and forgetting about the customers. Don't become engulfed with making the product/brand so excellent that you forget to add value and quality to your service, also look out for updates and changes to accommodate your changing market and demographic.

Your business is all about your customers, or clients, period. After all, your customers are the people that will ultimately decide if your business goes boom or bust. You can leave an imprint of care and excellence with each interaction with your customers/clients that will guarantee a reference or return. It's the make or breaker law with customers/clientele. Everything you do in business must be customer focused, including your policies, warranties, payment options, operating hours, presentations, advertising and promotional campaigns and website. In addition, you must know who your customers are inside out and upside down.

7.   *Marketing & Branding* – Every entrepreneur needs to brand his or herself. You need to define your brand by the quality and the service you bring. You also need to have a

unique image about your product or service that makes you stand out amid all the other companies who may be doing the self-same thing as you do. If you brand and market yourself correctly you will create a lasting impression as well as a memorable one. Out of all the companies your client can choose from they will always remember you.

You have to learn the art of self-promotion and not rely on hiring too many companies to do the talking and marketing for you. Also learn to market yourself without being obnoxious and annoying because customers will become easily turned off and look elsewhere to perform their business and duties. Along with your marketing you need to build a positive image about your business. Allow some of the truth and best qualities about your business to be highlighted in your marketing and branding. Remember to always project an image of excellence and professionalism.

8.   *Advance With Technology*- We live in a world that is changing all the time. Technology is improving all the time and the mom and pop way of doing business is slowly becoming a thing of the past. Entrepreneurs must balance how they approach adding technology to their business by adding changes when necessary

but not going overboard. It's OK to explore new options as they become available but as long as they fit your brand and your image. Never use something that will make you look like a misfit.

9.   *Every Business Needs A Team* There are no super heroes when it comes to entrepreneurship. One of the tell-tell signs of a business headed for failure is a business without a team, support or partnerships. Even if you are operation a s-corp. (sole proprietorship) where you are the only owner, you will still need to contract workers to provide services and partner with people to make accomplishments that you're unable to do. Or even hire people to work under you while you attend to other areas of the business. The point is you need a team!

No one person can build a successful business completely alone. You will need people that are as committed as you are to making sure the business succeeds in its endeavors. People who are as passionate about your work as you are and take the company seriously. Your business team may include family members, friends, suppliers, business alliances, employees, sub-contractors, industry and business associations, local government and the community.

Last but definitely not the least is your customers and clients are among the most important people apart of your team. Your customers are the deciding factor on the changes, progression, success, failure and future of the business, they encompass that much power!

The Newborn Entrepreneur

The Laws of Entrepreneurship II

Chapter Eleven:

10. *Become known as an expert.*

When you have a problem that needs to be solved, do you seek just anyone's advice or do you seek an expert in the field to help solve your particular problem? Obviously, you want the most accurate information and assistance that you can get. You naturally seek an expert to help solve your problem. You call a plumber when your pipes leak, a real estate agent when it's time to sell your home or a dentist when you have a toothache. Therefore, it only stands to reason that the more you become known for your expertise in your business, the more people will seek you out to tap into your expertise, creating more selling and referral opportunities.

When I first began working on writing out tips, ideas, strategies and concepts to help other authors improve their work I had already begun to receive calls requesting my insight and input on peoples projects. People began to watch my work and my work was speaking for me. People took note that I kept publishing books and with each book came some significant strides in my success. You can achieve the same by working on your expertise and forming it into a business or product/service that can be sold. In effect, becoming known as an expert is another style of prospecting for new business, just in reverse. Instead of finding new and qualified people to sell to, these people seek you out for your expertise.

11. *Create a competitive advantage.*
A home business must have a clearly defined unique selling proposition. This is nothing more than a fancy way of asking the vital question, "Why will people choose to do business with you or purchase your product or service instead of doing business with a competitor and buying his product or service?" In other words, what one aspect or combination of aspects is going to separate your business from your competition? Will it be better service, a longer warranty, better selection, longer business hours, more flexible payment options, lowest price, personalized service,

better customer service, better return and exchange policies or a combination of several of these? These were some of the determining factors I had to place together along with my business plan for reaching my success.

12.   *Invest in yourself.*

You have to learn how to invest in your mind. Purchasing educational material that will help you build your expertise as well as your skills and abilities. Top entrepreneurs buy and read business and marketing books, magazines, reports, journals, newsletters, websites and industry publications, knowing that these resources will improve their understanding of business and marketing functions and skills. At first I must admit that it took me a while to get into the swing of investing into reading materials and magazines.

Join business associations and clubs, and network with other skilled business people to learn their secrets of success and help define their own goals and objectives. Top entrepreneurs attend business and marketing seminars, workshops and training courses, even if they have already mastered the subject matter of the event. They do this because they know that education is an ongoing process. There are usually ways to do things better, in less time, with less effort. In short, top entrepreneurs never stop investing in the most powerful, effective and best business and marketing tool at their immediate disposal--themselves. Staying connected to key organizations and institutions is key.

13. *Be accessible.*

We're living in a time when we all expect our fast food lunch at the drive-thru window to be ready in mere minutes, our money to be available at the cash machine and our pizza delivered in 30 minutes or it's free. Most of us can find ourselves being impatient at times, not wanting to stand on lines and wait or expecting instant service were ever we go. Realistically, we live in a spoiled society receiving instant service may not always be possible. You see the pattern developing--you must make it as easy as you can for people to do business with you, regardless of the home business you operate.

14. *Considerate of Client's Needs*

You must remain cognizant of the fact that few people will work hard, go out of their way, or be inconvenienced just for the privilege of giving you their hard-earned money. The shoe is always on the other foot. Making it easy for people to do business with you means that you must be accessible and knowledgeable about your products and services. You must be able to provide customers with what they want, when they want it. Customer service is not always an easy task, you may feel a customer is spoiled, a complainer or looking for a free deal. No matter if the case is true or not, sometimes it's not worth risking your sales or losing a loyal customer over small things, such as a coupon, free shipping or a free item that may have been promised as a deal. Remember to remain considerate.

15. *Build A Firm Reputation.*

A good reputation is unquestionably one of the home business owner's most tangible and marketable assets. People need to know that your service or product is reliable. They also need to know that you provide outstanding service to your customers or clients with their best interest at heart. You can't simply buy a good reputation; it's something that you earn by honoring your promises. If you promise to have the merchandise in the customer's hands by Wednesday, you have no excuse not to have it there. If you offer to repair something, you need to make good on your offer. Consistency in what you offer is the other key factor. If you cannot come through with the same level of service (and products) for clients on a regular basis, they have no reason to trust you . . . and without trust, you won't have a good reputation.

16.   *Sell yourself & Sell benefits.*

Entrepreneurship is the only business where it's ok to sell yourself! When it comes to making money beyond the traditional 9-5 job many people are mastering and learning the art of becoming a product. Becoming a product means that you make yourself a brand to your consumers. People buy into you because they believe in your vision and your leadership. That's what sets the entrepreneur markets standards. That's why you can have hundreds of companies selling products and they are all making money. That should tell the neonate entrepreneur something, "there's enough money out there for all of us!"

Pushing product features is for inexperienced or wannabe entrepreneurs. Selling the benefits associated with owning and using the products and services you carry is what sales professionals worldwide focus on to create buying excitement and to sell, sell more, and sell more frequently to their customers. Your advertising, sales presentations, printed marketing materials, product packaging, website, newsletters, trade show exhibit and signage are vital. Every time and every medium used to communicate with your target audience must always be selling the benefits associated with owning your product or using your service.

17.   *Get Involved.*

Always go out of your way to get involved in the community that supports your business. You can do this in many ways, such as pitching in to help local charities, nonprofits or the food bank, becoming involved in organizing community events, and getting involved in local politics. You can join associations and clubs that concentrate on programs and policies designed to improve the local community. It's a fact that people like to do business with people they know, like and respect, and with people who do things to help them as members of the community.

18.   *Grab Attention.*

Small-business owners cannot waste time, money and energy on promotional activities aimed at building awareness solely through long-term, repeated exposure. If you do, chances are you will go broke long before this goal is accomplished. Instead, every promotional activity you engage in must put money back in your pocket so that you can continue to grab more attention and grow your business. Find new creative ways to spark the interest of you clients. Take advantage of any free marketing and resources opportunities such as social media, YouTube, get clients to post testimonials and reviews of your products or services to boost your exposure and reputation.

19. *Master the art of Negotiations.*

The ability to negotiate effectively is unquestionably a skill that every home business owner must make every effort to master. Negotiation comes in handy when making deals where your company has to spend money and it's also a skill that is profitable to have when customers know they can take their dollars elsewhere. Having the ability to negotiate can empower you to earn new clients, keep old clients and grow in profits. Negotiating perhaps second in importance only to asking for the sale in terms of home business musts. In business, negotiation skills are used daily. Always remember that mastering the art of negotiation means that your skills are so finely tuned that you can always orchestrate a win-win situation. These win-win arrangements mean that everyone involved feels they have won, which is really the basis for building long-term and profitable business relationships.

20. *Design your workspace for success.*

Carefully plan and design your home office workspace to ensure maximum personal performance and productivity and, if necessary, to project professionalism for visiting clients. If at all possible, resist the temptation to turn a corner of the living room or your bedroom into your office. Set up a space that gives you your own work space that's more appropriate and friendly for people to come and conduct business with you. Ideally, you'll want a separate room with a door that closes to keep business activities in and family members out, at least during prime business and revenue generating hours of the day. A den, spare bedroom, basement or converted garage are all ideal candidates for your new home office. If this is not possible, you'll have to find a means of converting a room with a partition or simply find hours to do the bulk of your work when nobody else is home where you will not run into disturbances and distractions.

21. *Get and stay organized.*

The key to staying organized is not about which type of file you have or whether you keep a stack or two of papers on your desk, but it's about managing your business. It's about having systems in place to do things. Therefore, you want to establish a routine by which you can accomplish as much as possible in a given workday, whether that's three hours for a part-time business or seven or nine hours as a full-timer.

In fact, you should develop systems and routines for just about every single business activity. Small things such as creating a to-do list at the end of each business day, or for the week, will help keep you on top of important tasks to tackle. Creating a single calendar to work from, not multiple sets for individual tasks or jobs, will also ensure that jobs are completed on schedule and appointments kept. Incorporating family and personal activities into your work calendar is also critical so that you work and plan from a single calendar. Once you have all of your activities and objectives in order it will be easy to manage what your day to day task and responsibilities are. Making time for family, the wife, husband or kids is very important. You don't want to spend so much time building your business that you neglect the people you love and support what you do. Even making time to be social is important, meeting with friends, mentors and associates that are supportive of you or just for social entertainment.

22. *Take time off.*

The temptation to work around the clock is very real for some home business owners. There are many entrepreneurs that dive head into their business without considering some of the pointers I ended with in number 21 of the laws of entrepreneurship. After all, you don't have a manager telling you it's time to go home because they can't afford the overtime pay. Every person working from home must take time to establish a regular work schedule that includes time to stretch your legs and take lunch breaks, plus some days off and scheduled vacations.

Create the schedule as soon as you have made the commitment to start a home business. Of course, your schedule will have to be flexible. You should, therefore, not fill every possible hour in the day. Give yourself a backup hour or two. All work and no play makes you burn out very fast and cantankerous customer service is not what people want.

23. *Limit the number of hats you wear.*

It's difficult for most business owners not to take a hands-on approach. They try to do as much as possible and tackle as many tasks as possible in their business. The ability to multitask, in fact, is a common trait shared by successful entrepreneurs. However, once in a while you have to stand back and look beyond today to determine what's in the best interest of your business and yourself over the long run. I can personally tell you from a wealth of business experience, you cannot do it all yourself. Not only that but you must learn how to relinquish responsibilities to other staff members as well as train others to handle tasks that can alleviate you and allow to accomplish more. Most highly successful entrepreneurs will tell you that from the time they started out, they knew what they were good at and what tasks to delegate to others.

24. *As for references*

When you provide your customers with excellent service you should not be afraid of asking for references or referrals. You should also ask for testimonials, written or by video. This will help in building credibility and attract loyal customers who will genuinely appreciate your service product. Asking your customers to refer other family members and friends to your business will help you to grow at a fast pace. Everyone in business knows that one of the most successful ways to quickly grow and market your business is through good services and word of mouth recommendations. Another helpful tip considering the type of service you provide asking for reference letters or testimonials of how your service has helped your client will help grow your business as well as help you to gain new clients.

25.   *Follow-up constantly.*

Constant contact, follow-up, and follow-through with customers, prospects, and business alliances should be the mantra of every home business owner, new or established. Constant and consistent follow-up enables you to turn prospects into customers, increase the value of each sale and buying frequency from existing customers, and build stronger business relationships with suppliers and your core business team. Follow-up is especially important with your existing customer base, as the real work begins after the sale. It's easy to sell one product or service, but it takes work to retain customers and keep them coming back.

The Newborn Entrepreneur

Let's Have A Conversation

Chapter Twelve:

"Progressiveness is looking forward intelligently, looking within critically, and moving on incessantly." Warren-

I want us to have a conversation; I want us to talk about where you are and where you're going. I want you to ask yourself these important questions that I am going to list further down into this chapter and when you're able to answer these questions be honest with yourself.

1. *Do you believe you have what it takes?*

I don't mean personal characteristics or not just personal characteristics, anyway. Do you believe you have all the skills, energy, money, people, and knowledge to start a business? You have to have the personal will power, confidence and belief that you're doing the right thing, know that the skill, service or product you're providing is worthwhile and have value. You have to love what you're doing and are sure it is something you won't fall out of love with or lackluster the motivation to be able to continue with it as time begins to pass.

Too many entrepreneurs start off on the course and take U-turns or run into burnout because it started off as a great idea but in the end they lack the staying power, skill, mind power and motivation to keep up with the demand of the business or the highs and lows that come along with it. You have to know with your own confidence that you have what it takes.

2.   *Decide what you want*

While it sounds like something simple so many people don't have a clue on what they want, they have ideas, they have goals, might have even set a few plans but no real "action". You have to get out of the "not knowing what to do with yourself syndrome" if you ever plan to be a successful entrepreneur. Taking the time to know what you want, how you're getting there, defining and refining your vision is what it will take to set you on course. One of the easiest ways to assist you in making a decision is to decide why you want to be in business? Why being in business is important to you. When you give yourself purpose behind what you're doing, it doesn't matter what comes along you can weather the storm until you make it to your expected end.

3. How do you handle setbacks?

When you are smiling, the whole company smiles with you. The way you carry yourself and the energy you carry makes a big difference when you're doing business. People can feel that energy who works with you and for you, your customers or clients feel it as well. Emotions are contagious: Morale rises and falls with the mood of the leader.

Consequently, people who succumb to black moods or depression can fatally infect their own companies. Taking the time to "take responsibility for the energy you bring into your work atmosphere is crucial". In order to ensure that you succeed at what you're doing leave any and all ill emotions to the side that may affect your performance while working. Because some people have an inflated idea of their resilience, I would suggests performing a kind of reference check on yourself -- ask people who know you well how you handle adversity. "If you are the type of person who needs to retreat for a period to recharge, that's not possible in these situations," "If you have a very high sense of responsibility and you take setbacks hard, you have to know that. Ask people to be honest about how they've seen you behave in hard times." Based on your character assessment from your peers you can build your own personal strategy as to how you will handle stress, depression, failure or loss. We all at some point experience it so it's pointless not to be prepared.

4. *What Skill Do You Use to Make Money?*

Now interestingly enough I hear allot of people say they don't have any special skill or talent that they could use to make them any extra money. If they were sitting with me in my office I would tell them that's not true, here's a few examples why. If you work a job period you have to have skills, so apparently you're already half way there. Your using skills to empower someone else's business but don't know how to empower yourself.

 You might be saying that was cute, but hit me with something else, well here it is, and you speak English don't you? Well, why not tutor someone in learning Basic English. You can do that while drinking your favorite Starbucks coffee and preparing your dinner. How about if you proficient at math, tutor struggling children or teens maybe even college adults for a little extra money. It's really that simple.

If you're a good singer or song writer, how about voice lessons for those who want to sing? To those who sing and desire to write; workshops to improve skills and performance, and how about teaching others how to write music of their own. Write some contracts and start writing songs for people and make money. You love to talk? Why not become a public speaker, since talking is a natural skill for you and comes easy, why not get paid to do it? I could go on and on with examples, even though some of these were small example's it can turn out to be something big and worthwhile for someone who has skill.

If you have a skill, no matter what it may be my advice to you would be to cultivate that skill further and use it for something that can earn you extra income. I love teaching and speaking before people and look where it has taken me. I am an author of several books on various topics and I love to teach. I love to empower people, that is a skill and people are in need of what I provide.

5. Can you accept that your company may outgrow you?

Some entrepreneurs love to brag that they don't need an exit strategy, because they are not going anywhere. But at some point, your business may need you less than you need it. That's particularly true at fast-growth companies, at which entrepreneurs may not have enough time to develop the necessary leadership and business skills.

When a company out grows its CEO or leading staff it may replace it by bringing in others to run the company and perform the necessary duties and tasks that are required. This can hurt a company whose CEO is not equipped or mature enough to know when to let go of his or her grip so the company can advance. Some look at it as if the company is advancing without them. After all, you still own the company and really have not lost any status or respect you're just abasing so someone more equipped and knowledgeable can come in and empower the company to go forward with the right skill, knowledge and fortitude needed to render success.

6. When you look in the mirror, does an entrepreneur look back?

From a child growing up I could never envision myself working a 9-5 job. I knew early on in life that entrepreneurship was something I was called to. When I looked in the mirror I could envision myself leading a company and setting order and giving demands. After getting over the egotistical side of things the reality set in that I would have to build skill that would allow me to lead the way I needed to. Not only that but prepare myself for the possibility of one day leading people who maybe just as knowledgeable as I and not to mention rub elbows with those who may even surpass my knowledge and there's no room for intimidation and being timid.

Entrepreneurship is something you have to enter with the right mindset or you will give up quickly and turn in your freedom papers to become a 9-5 slave. A 9-5 slave is a slave to a wage and you really have no freedom to explore your skills, gifts, talents and experience the world with balance and enjoyment. That's one of the gifts that entrepreneurship provides. When you look in the mirror do you see endurance? How long can you hang in there? Entrepreneurship is a calling, it's also a venture where it may take a few years to see significant results and it's not a get rich quick party.

Research into entrepreneurs' personal traits and you will find qualities like persistence, endurance, patience and need for achievement. The difference between people who start companies and those who don't is the exploration of achievement and the enhancement of personal skill and the lack of fear that makes the difference. People who choose not to go into business for themselves are less worried about wealth building, changing policies and strategies. They seem to fall in line with the spirit of the times, the economy, and changes within an industry. While the people who start business are a part of the reason those things evolve and change.

7. *Are You Willing to Create and Execute A Wealth Building Process?*
Wealth follows people who create, follow or institute a system in their lives. You have to be willing to submit yourself to a philosophy of entrepreneurship that works for you. Surround yourself with people who have attained the wealth and power that you are looking to attain to. Glean from their wisdom and

mentorship and apply the things that you learn as quickly as possible.

Understand that there is no quick way to get rich. If there were don't you think everyone would be wealthy? Now everyone has fallen prey to some get rich or wealthy scheme at some point in their lives. Real wealth is in a system of strategies that works to build a product, service or company. When applied correctly the results can be record breaking. Entrepreneurship is one of the only creative ventures that will allow you to create such wealth that not only makes history but leave a legacy.

Once you make a wealth building plan you have to stick to it. You have to develop a "stick to it-ness" attitude and not fall prey to desiring to change your plan when things don't look like what you want it to look like. You also have to develop an entrepreneur's intuition and allow it to mature and as it matures you will be able to navigate when change is of the necessity and when it is not.

The Newborn Entrepreneur

The Power of Entities

Chapter Thirteen:

If the only business you have is maintaining someone else business, then you have no business at all.
Michael McCain

If you want to be a successful entrepreneur you have to first ditch the "fake it till you make it theory". Or how about you all together just "stop acting rich" and learn what it really takes to build lasting wealth and be one of those who actually become rich. Below I am going to give you a list of things that will get you on the road to creating wealth and your financial dreams. This list is not in any specific order but can be used interchangeably as needed.

1. Save Money
2. Assets
3. Investments
4. Building Multiple Streams of Income
5. Live Within Your Means
6. Brand Yourself
7. Create Entities

8. Form Entities

Any business owner or millionaire will be able to tell you the power of entities and their effects on your finances. Entities are a valuable part of how you can grow your wealth and protect your wealth. The purposes of entities are to:

1. Maximize tax strategies
2. Create liability protection
3. Ensure asset protection
4. Keep your wealth accelerating through multiple streams of revenue
5. Optimize opportunities

There are six basic types of companies or entities that can help you grow your business as an entrepreneur as well as create, save and grow wealth. These entities are important for saving with taxes; it determines how a company pays its taxes and what a company can save from the benefits of what type of entity you have.

1. C Corporations

A C-Corp. is a standard business corporation and represents the most typical structure for-profit entity that pays taxes on the income it generates. The C refers to Subchapter C of the

IRS code, under which the corporation is taxed. When you form a C- Corp. you have formed a legal entity that is spate from yourself. C Corporations protects a person's personal assets shareholders have no personal liability for the corporations debts or actions. It acts on its own authority, it files its own taxes, and it can have an unlimited number of shareholders.

C corporations own their own assets, incur their own liabilities, and can provide goods or services. They meet the requirements for about 300 deductible expenses. The fiscal year is flexible and can end at any time. (More commonly most corporations that fall under this category usually end their calendar year at December 31st of each year).

C corporations are taxed on their operating income, and all dividends are considered taxable income; which means shareholders of C Corporations are often double taxed, the business pays taxes off its operating income and shareholders pay taxes off of the profits they have eared.

C corporations often receive benefits in the area of tax breaks depending on the state or existing laws at the time where the corporation exists. C corporations receive a low tax rate on the first 50,000 the company earns (this is an example of a basic benefit of a C corporation).

2.   S Corporation-
S corporations are typically small corporations with no more than 75 owners, like the C corporations, they are legal entities authorized by state law and protect shareholders from legal liability. They are often referred to as a Subchapter S, because they are taxed under Subchapter S of the IRS code.

S corporations pay no income tax. All profits and losses pass right through to the shareholders, who then assume liability for the taxes. The shareholders are not doubly taxed as they are in C corporations. S corporations meet the requirements for approximately 150 allowable expense deductions and can be used as a multi-corporation strategy. Most companies start at this level and later switch to a C corporation when the company grows and begins to earn higher earnings.

3.   Limited Partnership

A Limited Partnership is not a corporation but a business organization with one or more general partners and one or more limited partners. A limited partnership is a partnership that must be approved by the secretary of state where it is created. A limited partnership is distinguished between general partnerships, which are usually a separately taxed entity. In a separate taxed entity the corporation's partners are taxed because the profits pass through its partners. The partners file taxes and report losses on their individual returns.

In a Limited Partnership, the general partners are the active investors who manage the business and are liable for its financial debts and legal obligations. They are responsible for 100 percent of the assets they own. Limited partners are passive investors who share in the cash flow, but do not share in the authority of the business. The assets of a general partner are always at risk. All partners contribute to the finance of the business, either with cash or something of comparable value, such as property or equity.

4.   Family Limited Partnerships

Family Limited Partnerships (FLPs) are limited partnerships where the majority of the partners are family members, simply put. These are powerful entities created to help protect a family's assets as an estate-planning pool. FLP's are formed to pass down wealth to other family members such as grandparents to parents and then the next generation. These entities allow a family to pool their assets into a estate and give up their assets as well as pass them on to others in the family such as children and grandchildren or extended family. Children under the age of 14 are not taxed, when they exceed the age of 14 they will begin to take on the burden represented by their proportional ownership of the FLP.

5.   Limited Liability Company

Limited Liability Company (LLC) is neither a partnership nor corporation. This legal entity forms the best of both corporations and partnerships. A separate entity for liability protection, anyone who owns a LLC gains the personal privilege of protection from liability of LLC's debts, except to the extent of what they invest in the LLC. LLC participants are called members, theirs an elected managing member which makes the decisions on the behalf of the entity. An LLC is nearly identical to the tax set up and benefits of an S corporation, but the annual reporting requirements and other more flexible tax treatments make LLC's one the most popular of entity structures used today. People particularly use this structure for the protection of their assets and real estate investments.

6.   Trust

A trust is a legal structure that is used to hold legal title to property for the benefit of one or more persons. There are usually three parties to a trust:

1.   The trust creator or generator
2.   The trustee, the person or institution that holds legal title to the property.
3.   The beneficiary or beneficiaries who are intended to benefit from the trust.

A trust serves as a separate entity, used typically for estate planning, protection of assets. Many people form trust to protect their income from creditors and taxes. I would recommend that a trust be the umbrella to all your entities, removing yourself as the individual making money and putting your business in the position of making the money.

You can protect yourself, your income and assets this way.

I would recommend you to seek out a lawyer that can help you properly form these entities the ones that best fit your needs for business as well as protect your assets and income. You can own several entities of different types and use your trust to be an umbrella to these different corporations and entities. Keep in mind the tax benefits that are associated with each and how they may protect and serve your business.

The Power of Vision

Chapter Fourteen:

When you close your eyes where do you see yourself, when you open your eyes do you see your reality?
Michael McCain

Vision is one of the most powerful tools an entrepreneur has. Vision is the make and breaker component. A great vision can change your life and leave a lasting legacy. A struggling vision can lead you down a road of dead-ends and disappointments. The question to ask yourself is what do you see? As a matter of fact where do you see yourself? I often tell people if your waiting for someone to take you there, place you there or validate the gift or ability that is in you, you will be lost like a ship without a sail. Like a homeless man/woman without a friend.

As a leader and entrepreneur you have to put yourself where you see yourself. No one is going to do the work for you. Entrepreneurship is the awakening of that inner calling, yearning and bringing desire for more and for achievement. Some people start identifying that call by accident others take steps to prepare for it by working temporarily jobs that supply them with the financial means to explore their dreams and talents, but the answer simply is that you have to have vision.

Vision is the act or power of sensing with the eyes; or sight. Sometimes we can come across a great vision by dreaming or seeing a trend and developing our own spin on that idea or concept. At other times you will find that true vision requires you to step out on the invisible and as you begin to walk, things start manifesting this never before seen world before your eyes.

Have you ever seen someone do something as watch how fast the success of what they have done takes off and you begin to say to yourself "why didn't I think of that first." Or how about you thought of something creative but procrastinated so long someone else came along with the same idea and blueprint and you were left sore amazed at the similarities if not the fact that it completely mirrored your exact idea. There's a reason for that!

When the creator gives us ideas they come out the spirit and spirit holds no time, distance or body. Another spirit being like you can pick up when they are aligned correctly and postured to hear and take the idea and run with that concept. You'll be left in the dust feeling like you missed your opportunity, but in reality the idea that you had was just hanging in the universe and waiting for someone to pick it up and the truth be told more than one person can hear the same thing but chances are very few will act on it. So the question I want to ask you is what do you do with what you hear?

Vision is also defined as: the act or power of anticipating that which will or may come to be. When you have vision you really don't need any physical proof or backing if the thing exists. Entrepreneurs are known for developing and following what I like to call "the entrepreneurs intuition". It's that inner voice, that inner vision that you have where you know the end result and you know something can be accomplished and achieved and you set your face against the current to be able to make that thing happen.

Vision is having the ability to center yourself so that you can achieve your target goal, intention and purpose. Vision is the mission statement that's written within the entrepreneur's heart and seems to be infused in all the work that he or she does. Entrepreneurs see what no one else sees, creates opportunities that usually do not exist before the start and completion of their idea. True entrepreneurs are not afraid to blend out, entrepreneurs do not like to blend in with the trend, but they are also wise enough to work with others even a part of their same work skill to build knowledge and network with resources.

When you are a visionary you have to be quick witted and have the ability to pull together a team and know that you can't do everything on your own. You have to have an eye to be able to identify quality, excellence and be able to employ people to help you build your vision and bring it to pass. Use wisdom, because you cannot share your ideas with everyone. You should only be sharing your ideas with people that can solve your problem or give you guidance as to how to affect a plan or strategy. Never share your vision with ordinary people, lest you don't care about them plagiarizing your ideas and becoming your competition.

Visionaries are people in spite of the obstacles see the end result and work hard at the completion of their work because they know the effect that it will have. Visionaries are people who stand the test of time and at the completion celebrate but take little rest because at the place of arrival usually arrives the next goal or accomplishment at a milestone. Use wisdom and pace yourself. Erect a plan and blueprint for how you will carry out your affairs (we will get more into that in the next chapter).

The Newborn Entrepreneur

The Power of A Plan

Chapter Fifteen:

God smiles on the wisdom of a wise man and add grace to the way a fool for he made them both-
Michael McCain

As a neonate entrepreneur you need to develop a concrete plan for your business. I can remember when I started my publishing company and my professional services company; there was no greater feeling then when I held my business proposal and vision statement in my hand. It was not something I could share with everyone just to pass it around but it was the literal blueprint for the purpose and plans of my business. It was detailed and not only spoke of my plans for my business but even included some strategies for how I would carry out my plan and make sure that my business became successful.

No entrepreneur should start a business without having the following:

1.   Vision Statement

2. Mission Statement
3. Company Values
4. Proposal
5. Marketing Strategy
6. Estimated Cost or Projected Earnings
7. Demographic/ Target Market

When you take the time to write your vision out you take time to show the importance, the detail, the process, the goals that are before you and you can pace yourself as to how fast or how slow you are getting there. You have to keep in mind that no matter how fast or slow the success it is all a process. Your written out vision will allow you to see your expected end even when things look like they are opposing your success. It sets the president for what your standard is and what you're fighting to accomplish and achieve as a newborn or reoccurring entrepreneur.

As the saying go's; "no plan, plan to fail". No one wants to start a business and fail. That's why a plan/ business proposal needs to be among the first steps to the foundation of building your business. That all comes together after you have done your research, count up the cost, learned your information and you're demographic. Once you have that information in place you begin build your plan, strategies and budget for your business.

Your business plan puts clear goals and objectives before you. It allows you to know the plan and direction your desire to take your company. Beyond that it adds professionalism as well as empowers you to know what to ask for and who is able to help you reach your goals. When you sit with investors they want to see your plan and know before cutting a check that you are a worthwhile investment.

I strongly suggest to any entrepreneur to start here. Set up your plan, your purpose, your vision statements and business plan. Make sure you cover all the things in the list I shared with you. It will save you money, time and energy. You will know where to focus your best efforts and dollars to grow your new business.

The Newborn Entrepreneur

Final Words

I know that this book has empowered and enlighten many. My goal with this book was not to make myself an expert but to share what I have learned over the years of developing and mentoring businesses. I have made many mistakes over the years and I am presently growing companies that are turning a profit.

It took me years to reach the place where I am now, I want to be sure that along the way I share the wisdom that I have gained and help someone else to achieve success. In this instance if you truly follow the pattern, the tips, the outlines and strategies given in this book to grow your business you will find that you have emerged into a powerful and successful entrepreneur.

Over time you will learn that it literally takes a network of people to make a business successful. You have to find the experts and the people who are serious about helping business profit and save money. People who are willing to teach you what they know and help you advance to another level. This even includes yourself when you have reached the hallmark of your desires. Never forget where you have come from. You should reach out to people and extend the wisdom you have learned to help others reach their success.

This means you need mentors, you need accountants, and you need experts in your field which are willing to share with you what they know. You have to also understand that sometimes it means you have to pay people for their expertise. Know that everything will not always be free. In the business world you have to respect people's knowledge. How would you feel if someone used you for everything you know and never offer you anything? This is not the way to build relationships and partnerships. Even if a person has not asked for payment, it's important to offer them something for their time. Maybe even treat them to a dinner or something as a gesture of appreciation. This will help you establish lasting relationships and people will know that you are a serious entrepreneur.

Take the wisdom in this book and build yourself a fortune 500 company! It's in you! You can do it. You may not make it to a fortune 500 company but it does not mean that you should not run your business with excellence and have things in order that will help assure that you prosper.

Congratulations on completing the newborn entrepreneur book. Share this book with any person you know looking to start a business or company. I encourage you to post your testimonials, videos and feedback to any social media website. I especially encourage you to post your reviews to amazon, Barnes and Noble as well as videos to YouTube and other video sharing websites. Now go grow your business!

The Newborn Entrepreneur

Other Books By The Author

1. Soul Cleanse Vol. 1 (Poetry)

2. Lost & Found (Poetry)

3. Life Editing Vol. 1- Taking Out The Trash

4. Called To Affluence

5. Diary Of An Ex Husband

6. Wealth & Abundance (Meditations for Prosperous Living)

7. The Millionaire Class Vol. 1

8. Prayerology Vol. 1- The School Of Prayer

9. The Purpose Driven Prayer Life

The Newborn Entrepreneur

About The Author

Dr. Michael McCain, best known as a motivational speaker, author. Yet there's more to his experience and story Dr. McCain is also a poet, entrepreneur, life coach and spiritual teacher. Michael is also an established author of several books over the last 10 years and has grown in his experience to go from print press publishing to owning his own publishing company. Michael has a wide range of experience both in business and in the non-profit religious sector. Best known as the General in the Art of Strategic Prayer and Spiritual Warfare, The Author of "Prayerology" Michael McCain is a life coach, Prophetic voice and Ambassador of Hope.

Dr. Michael McCain is a 21st Century World Leader who has partnered with business moguls, politicians, church, civic and world leaders for more than 15 years to equip and empower millions to maximize their potential. As one of the leading voices of our time, he founded Dr. Michael McCain Enterprises Inc. (DMME), Maximize Publishing Inc. & Kaleo University, as well as a conglomerate of companies and business to bring practical solutions to spiritual and social ills; effecting change within our communities while transforming the course of our global destiny. His track record as a revolutionary thinker and prolific communicator, has established him as one of the most respected and sought–after youthful leaders in the world today.

Since 2010 Michael McCain has been a highly sought–after spiritual coach mentoring leaders, clergy and lay members. With his move in the publishing industry he has set himself apart not just to the church but to the world; making his life coaching experience broad enough to reach people in the pews as well as the secular marketplace. He has successfully made his mark with his books in Self Help and Empowerment as well as Spirituality and Entrepreneurship. His wisdom as insight is beyond his years and is a voice that will be remembered through generations.